Puppy Socialization

An Insider's Guide to Dog Behavioral Fitness

Caryl Wolff,
(Yes, that's my real name!)
Certified Dog Behavior Consultant

Testimonials

What others are saying about this book:

This is a great book. Caryl has mastered the art of deftly marrying comprehensive scientific principles with reader accessibility, no easy task. Puppy Socialization is a treasure trove of information and puppies around the world are breathing a sigh of relief that it has been published. This book deserves a top shelf placement among the thousands of puppy and dog books ever written. And the cover photo alone is worth the price of admission.

Paul Owens
The Original Dog Whisperer

◆◆◆◆◆◆◆◆◆◆◆◆◆◆

Neurologists are learning the importance of early development for brain health in dogs. It's great to see this subject addressed in a concise, well organized new book on early puppy socialization. Caryl Wolff is a compassionate, competent and funny professional. This book is a must buy for new puppy owners and breeders.

Richard E. Palmquist, DVM
Centinela Animal Hospital

◆◆◆◆◆◆◆◆◆◆◆◆◆◆

Wow. "Comprehensive" doesn't even begin to do this book justice. Caryl has written a go-to socialization primer for anyone looking for it all in one place, be they dog pro, breeder, rescue org, or proud new puppy guardian. The whats and whys, facts and fictions, science and research, and the all-important how-to's are all right here.

Veronica Boutelle
dog*tec Founder and President

♦♦♦♦♦♦♦♦♦♦♦♦♦♦

This book has exhaustive information with terrific checklists and exercises that will be of great benefit not only to owners but also savvy breeders and rescue organizations.

Amy Shojai
Award-winning Author of 27 Pet Care Books
and Columnist on About.com for Dogs and Cats

♦♦♦♦♦♦♦♦♦♦♦♦♦♦

Puppy Socialization: An Insider's Guide to Dog Behavioral Fitness is more than a book, it is a tool to be used over and over for anyone who has or ever will encounter a puppy in their lives. From covering theory, research, and experts to providing checklists, how-to's and examples, Caryl Wolff unravels the many facets of socializing a puppy.

What I liked about this book is that you really do not have to read it front to back, though I would recommend doing so. It is laid out in clear chapters around: "who" is reading, "why" and "when." I can't recommend this book enough.

Cheryl Aguiar, PhD
Founder and Owner, E-Training for Dogs

♦♦♦♦♦♦♦♦♦♦♦♦♦♦

Caryl did a great job with this book. I like its being split in three sections -- one for breeders, one for owners, and one for rescue organizations -- and I love, love, love to read about puppy developmental periods and fear development. This is something that is missing in many other books. It's a great book that I will recommend to anyone with a puppy!

Corinne Kaelin, owner of dog-ibox.com,
the all-in-one solution for dog trainers
offering continuing education
and a dog trainer software

◆◆◆◆◆◆◆◆◆◆◆◆◆◆

I think the Puppy Socialization Guide is great for breeders because gives a lot of great info and also a breeder timeline. Breeders can then recommend to owners to continue what they have been doing. Then it is great for owners because it is easy to read.

I think if people can get a glimpse into early socialization and how important it is, it will help them as an owner - not just with small pups but with older dogs, too. While the book is geared towards younger dogs, it can help with older, newly adopted, etc. because it has can easily be directed towards later dogs in later developmental stages. I don't know that I've found one that has done it as easily as yours has.

I would also recommend it to trainers because I think it also gives the info in a great progression for them to gear puppy classes to. So it isn't an "owner only" or "breeder only" type of book -- it's good for everyone.

Nicole McBride
Certified Trainer & Obedience Instructor
through NADOI #1083. CGC & TDI Evaluator

◆◆◆◆◆◆◆◆◆◆◆◆◆◆

I love this book. It is clear, concise, friendly, and filled with terrific advice and ideas. The socialization check list is brilliant. I wish I had even half the knowledge she imparted when my dog was a puppy. Her love of dogs, her firm, but gentle methods, years of experience and sense of humor is the thread that ties the whole book together. She is like a doting mother for not only her children, but all children. She emphasizes the similarities and differences among dogs in terms of their personalities and how they react to other dogs and people. It's totally okay not to fit into a mold, but it is totally not okay to misbehave and be a bully. That goes for how people interact with dogs as well. Her analogies, thoughts, feelings and suggestions will surely be helpful and welcome to anyone with a new puppy and possibly even with an older dog.

Barbie B.

♦♦♦♦♦♦♦♦♦♦♦♦♦♦

Ever since I took my first dog to Caryl and saw the fantastic work that she does with training and socialization, I have brought all of my dogs to her. She truly is a wealth of information, and the Puppy Socialization Guide is a reflection of that. It's been about 10yrs now, and I have been happy to refer all of my new pet owner friends to her and will definitely encourage them to buy her book.

Velika Turner

PUPPY SOCIALIZATION:

An Insider's Guide to Dog Behavioral Fitness

Caryl Wolff,
Certified Dog Behavior Consultant

Copyright © 2014 by Caryl Wolff
ISBN-13: 978-1500181901
ISBN-10: 1500181900

Photos courtesy of
Meir Bartur
Laurel Cook and Ross McLaughlin
Fresh Patch
GoGoDogPals

Cover photo – www.bigstockphoto.com

Disclaimer and Warning

The author has made every effort to be as complete and accurate as possible regarding the information in this book at the time of printing and publishing. However, there may be both typographical and content mistakes. Additionally, there are other sources of material which cover other aspects of this subject or approach it in a different manner. Therefore, the reader should read other material, use the information in this book as a guide, and tailor it to his or her needs rather than rely on it as the ultimate source.

The author and publisher do not represent or warrant the completeness of the information in this book. They do not assume and they disclaim any liability to any party for any loss, disruption, or damage, including but not limited to special, incidental, consequential, or other damages caused or alleged to have been caused directly or indirectly by errors or omissions, whether such errors or omissions result from negligence, accident, or any other cause. The recommendations, advice, suggestions, and strategies contained herein may not be suitable for every situation.

Any organizations, websites, links, other books, or products referred to herein are for informational purposes only, and those references are not warranted for content, accuracy, or any other implied or explicit purpose. Citing references does not mean that the author or the publisher endorses any or all of the information that those references give or recommendations they make. Furthermore, those references may have changed or been removed between the time when this book was written and the time of reading.

This book is for information only and is not intended as a substitute for veterinary, grooming, dog training, or dog behavior advice or treatment. The reader should consult a veterinarian in matters relating to his or her dog's health and particularly with respect to any symptoms that may require diagnosis or medical attention, a groomer for grooming issues, a dog trainer for dog training issues, and a dog behavior consultant for dog behavior issues. If the reader does not wish to be bound by the above, then the reader may return this book to the publisher for a full refund.

Other books by Caryl Wolff:

Puppy Potty Training: The Expert's Guide to Easy Housetraining FAST

Teacup Puppies and Dogs: Choosing a Breeder & Choosing a Dog

Teacup Puppies and Dogs: Supplies, Pre-Puppy Prep & First Week Home

Teacup Puppies and Dogs: Feeding, Care, Safety, Health & Grooming

Teacup Puppies and Dogs: Obedience Training, Games & Play

Teacup Puppies and Dogs: Potty Training & Behavior Issues

Websites owned by Caryl Wolff

http://www.PuppySocializationGuide.com

http://www.puppy-dog-potty-training.com

http://www.DogBooksLibrary.com

http://www.DogSeminarsDirectory.com

http://www.DoggieManners.com

http://www.TeacupPuppiesAndDogs.com

http://www.DogTrainersDirectory.com

http://www.los-angeles-rescue-dog-adoption.com

For the dogs in shelters
whose only "crime"
was not having proper socialization

Preface

(For ease, throughout this book, when
I'm talking about people in general, I'm
going to use "she" and "her" even
though there may be men involved, and
I will use "he," "his," and "him" when I'm
talking about dogs. And the breeder
sells the puppies to an owner because
it's too awkward to say "owner/guardian"
each time – and I'm old enough that
people were called "owners" before they
were called "guardians," so it's force of
habit. Finally, I will lump shelters and
rescuers under "rescues." I apologize in
advance if any of that offends anyone.)

I have been a dog trainer/behavior consultant for 20+ years
and have seen thousands of puppies in my career. I can tell
pretty quickly which puppies are going to be behaviorally fit
and which are not. The ones who are going to be fit, generally
speaking, have had breeders who breed dogs with solid
temperaments and/or rescue organizations who work with
them prior to the time that owners get them.

To me, the single most important factor in choosing a puppy
is choosing a breeder (or rescue) that has interacted with the
puppies similar to the methods outlined in this book. If the
breeder or rescue has not, then you will likely have a project
instead of a pet. I have owned several dogs in my life, all of
them rescued from shelters and rescue organizations, and
many of them were projects. I loved them all equally, but I
liked some more than others because they were easier to live
with.

If I were getting a new puppy, here's what I would do. First, I would research the breed's adult size, temperament, grooming, etc. (There are numerous checklists on the Internet to see if the puppy you want is actually compatible with your lifestyle, and that is outside the scope of this book. But I urge you to check those.) I would never get a puppy over the Internet unless the breeder has been highly recommended and I have carefully done research by corresponding with the breeder, contacting references, etc.

Then I'd look at pictures of the puppies and finally go to the breeder's facility (that hopefully is a house where the puppies are raised inside) and look at how the puppies are kept. What I don't want to see are lots of kennels with puppies playing together – huh? Yes, I want the place to be clean and to see the puppies playing, but I want to see more things in the kennels – balls, toys, ramps, and many of the other things I'm going to be talking about in this book. I would much rather purchase from a breeder who has the puppies in her house so I can see specifically where the puppies are raised and also meet the dam (mother) to see her temperament because a fearful or aggressive mother is likely to have fearful or aggressive puppies. It's all right for the litter to stay outdoors when the weather is appropriate, but I personally would want a puppy that spends most of his time in the house because that puppy has a head start on living in a house with all the sounds, smells, and activities that occur there vs. a puppy that lives in a kennel that has not experienced these things.

Trust me, it's not enough to be cute. No one gets a puppy anticipating it's going to be a behavior problem – we all want dogs that we can enjoy living with. If they're too much of a problem – well, the shelters are full of problem dogs.

Please don't interpret this to mean that every shelter dog is a problem dog because some dogs wind up in shelters because of a death in the family, the owners move, the owner's finances change. Here's a staggering statistic – half of the dogs born in the US every year are not alive by their second birthday. The majority of those dogs were euthanized because of behavior problems either because of poor breeding, poor rearing (lack of socialization and habituation), and lack of training.

The fact that you're reading this book means that you care enough so that your puppy will not be one of those sad statistics. I would encourage you to read the entire book, not just the section that pertains to you. The Breeder section primarily but not exclusively pertains to Breeders, and the same holds true for the Owner/Guardian section and the Rescue section. You will get ideas that you can easily incorporate into your daily routine.

One final thought – this is my seventh book. Small portions of this book were taken from my other books and incorporated into this one.

Pat yourself on the back, and enjoy the book!

Table of Contents

About the Author

Caryl Wolff has been training dogs and their people for over 20 years. (That is her birth name – was she destined to be a dog trainer?) She is the first dog trainer/behavior consultant concurrently certified by five dog trainer organizations –

- The International Association of Animal Behavior Consultants
- Certification Council for Professional Dog Trainers
- National Association of Dog Obedience Instructors
- Association of Animal Behavior Professionals,
- The American Kennel Club Canine Good Citizen Evaluator.

She has worked with thousands of dogs and puppies – and people. She loves to work with puppies and wants to make their lives better in order to keep them in their homes. She has seen firsthand the difference between puppies who come from breeders or rescue organizations who work with them and those who do not.

She has a wicked sense of humor and lives in Los Angeles with two dogs and a 42-year-old macaw, which she humorously refers to as her longest relationship.

Acknowledgements

I cannot thank people enough for helping me in writing this book. The first person is **Dr. Ed Bailey, B.S., M.S., Ph.D., Professor Emeritus, Animal Behavior University of Guelph**. I had read some of his articles, which appear here http://www.trader.co.nz/versatiledogs/behaviour.htm. Then I emailed him and asked for his comments. He went well beyond responding. I wish I had been able to study with him when I was starting out my career.

I am very grateful to the following people who have graciously permitted me to include articles written by each of them in this book:

- **Dr. Ian Dunbar** http://www.dogstardaily.com,
- **Dr. Carmen Battaglia** http://breedingbetterdogs.com
- **Peter and Nancy Vollmer** http://www.superpuppy.com (and the AKC Gazette)
- **Dr. Michael Fox** www.drfoxvet.com, kindly helped in setting the record straight about research.

Dr. Richard Palmquist, chief of integrative health services at Centinela Animal Hospital http://www.lovapet.com, past president and research chair of the American Holistic Veterinary Medical Association and president of the AHVM Foundation, Huffington Post contributor, and consultant for the Veterinary Information Network (VIN) encouraged me more than I could ever have imagined.

Adrienne Farricelli http://www.roversranchhome.com proofread the book and found mistakes that SpellCheck and another program did not find, and she also permitted me to use her article on puppy license. Thank you so very much!

Laurel Cook and Ross McLaughlin of Culandubh Kennels in Ontario, Canada http://www.foxredlabs.ca have provided the fabulous photos of their puppy area.

I so appreciate the comments about breeding from **Kristin Hotti** www.Goldengatelabradoodles.com .

Nicole McBride www.WoofsofWisdom.com read and critiqued the manuscript and made some valuable suggestions.

Dr. Claudeen McAuliffe of the Humane Animal Welfare Society http://hawspets.org/ kindly provided a portion of their handbook regarding socialization.

Meir Bartur let me use some adorable photos of his puppies.

I wish I could have included the comments and suggestions of everyone who has helped in the writing of this book. Thank you all so very much.

Lynn Conger http://www.silverkennel.com

Velika Turner http://www.realestatebyvelika.com

Barbie Barak

And most of all, I would like to thank **Sukru Boztepe,** my computer guru, who has helped with not only technical issues with the computer (and there were so many of them that I lost count) but also with encouraging me. He is a genius whose understanding of the technical is only exceeded by his patience and compassion. I could not have written this book without him.

INTRODUCTION

Chapter 1

This scope of this book is puppy socialization, habituation, and environmental enrichment – exposing puppies to new situations and their adapting to it before puberty. I may mention other aspects of puppy development as it relates to socialization but not give specific instructions on how to do it. For example, I may mention housetraining, but I've written an entire book on housetraining, so you can refer to that for specifics on housetraining.

The book is divided into three sections – one for breeders, one for owners, and one for rescues – but they all overlap, and the classifications are my way of sorting my thoughts. I encourage you to read the entire book. Trainers will also benefit from this book because they will get ideas to help their clients. Even though I've been training a long time, I learned a great deal from writing it because of the research – for example, some long-held beliefs had been modified or disproved.

This book is important because puppies who are not well socialized and habituated before 16 weeks old will not reach their full potential as adult dogs. You will learn what to do to help them as well as when and how to do it. The ultimate result is that your puppy will grow up to be a behaviorally fit dog.

This book is written for healthy normal puppies. If you have a puppy that has any medical condition, then get that tended to first. Your first duty is to the health of the puppies. Try to adapt the exercises whenever you can. You can still do many of the exercises in this book.

Anytime anyone writes a book, there is a general idea of what is going to be covered and then specifics on what information to include. I have communicated with breeders, owners, trainers, behavior consultants, and scientists as well as researched socialization. The information in this book is the product of that work. The tricky part is what to include and what to leave out. I could write forever and include everything I know and all the thousands of pages of notes about puppies. But I won't. Aren't you lucky?

If you would like a hard copy of the Owner's Checklist so you can actually check items off, please email me at caryl@PuppySocializationGuide.com.

Please send me an email with your suggestions on how to make the second edition better! I not only appreciate but welcome your comments, both good and bad. And I hope you like the book and will leave a review where you purchased it!

Thank you.

But let's answer the question:

What is Socialization and When Does It Start?

The term "socialization" has several definitions depending on where we look, and there is no single standard definition either in dictionaries or in academic disciplines. Merriam-Webster's dictionary defines "socialization" as "the process by which a human being beginning at infancy acquires the habits, beliefs, and accumulated knowledge of society through education and training for adult status." Wikipedia says it is "the lifelong process of inheriting and disseminating norms, customs, and ideologies providing an individual with the skills and habits necessary for participating within his or her own society." Steven Lindsay in The Handbook of Applied Dog Behavior and Training defines it as "learning to relate and communicate."

When **dog owners** speak about "socialization," they generally mean they want their puppy to get along with people and other dogs.

Dog trainers along with some **certified animal behaviorists** and **veterinary behaviorists** have a different definition of socialization.

Here is a portion of the AVSA position statement on puppy socialization:

> "The primary and most important time for puppy socialization is the first three months of life. During

this time puppies should be exposed to as many new people, animals, stimuli and environments as can be achieved safely"......

R.K. Anderson, a Diplomate of the American College of Veterinary Behaviorists, wrote the following letter to his fellow veterinarians:

"Puppies begin learning at birth and their brains appear to be particularly responsive to learning and retaining experiences that are encountered during the first 13 to 16 weeks after birth. This means that breeders, new puppy owners, veterinarians, trainers and behaviorists have a responsibility to assist in providing these learning/socialization experiences with other puppies/dogs, with children/adults and with various environmental situations during this optimal period from birth to 16 weeks." [The complete text of this letter appears later in this book.]

Even though those are their statements, in actuality, there are really two processes at work – socialization where a dog learns how to become a dog, and habituation where he learns how to live in his environment. Primary socialization is when the puppy learns how to be a dog. I'm emphasizing that this is primary socialization. Secondary socialization is really associative learning (where the puppy makes a connection two events) when the puppy gets used to things in the environment, including humans and other animals. Trainers, some certified animal behaviorists, and some veterinary behaviorists have blurred these two processes together and call it "socialization."

The definition of "socialization" for **animal behaviorists** is how an animal learns to interact socially with animals of its own species. For dogs, the period of primary socialization begins while he is still in the womb through chemical communication with the mother and ends at about fourteen weeks old. Secondary socialization occurs during the same time window when an animal learns to interact with another species, i.e., dogs to humans, cats, birds, etc.

I have read the articles by and have been in correspondence with **Dr. Ed Bailey** MSc. PhD. Professor Emeritus Animal Behavior - University of Guelph. He has been a great help in defining and discussing terminology. What follows is a summary of pertinent portions of his articles and our correspondence.

"I am concerned about the uses – and abuses – of the terms 'socialize' and 'socializing.' Most people are using 'socializing' and 'socialization' interchangeably and that is wrong. The two things are totally different. The implication is that socialize equals socialization. The use or rather the misuse of the word is the biggest myth of the whole thing.

"My article 'Socialization, Bonding and Socializing' in Gun Dog Magazine 1997. vol.17, no.1. pp 54-57 explains exactly the correct meaning of the terms and talks about the misuse.

"To me 'socializing' is two or more animals, almost always of the same species, interacting socially so as to result in a behavioral change in at least one of them. The term 'socializing' should not be taken as the verb form of the noun 'socialization.' It is incorrect to say you are 'socializing' a dog. Socializing in dogs means the same thing as it means in people. Two or more dogs doing almost anything together, engaged in any social activity, are socializing. Socializing is a 'with' rather than an 'on' or a 'to.' Socializing is putting to work the social skills acquired during socialization. Socialization is a process that is restricted to a short finite period early in an animal's life during which the animal learns how to interact socially with members of its own species. Socializing is a social interaction, and it occurs throughout the life of the animal.

"Two dogs smelling anal areas of each other is socializing. Two or three guys having a beer or six while watching an NFL Game is socializing. Two girls putting their heads together over Starbucks lattes are socializing. Walking a dog around Home Depot meeting lots of people is not socializing any more than, as one person wrote, 'getting a dog used to a crate is socializing the dog to the crate.' (I will forever feel deprived not ever witnessing the social interactions between a dog and his crate.) [My comment – Dr. Bailey is very funny!] Why not be behaviorally correct and call it habituation which is what it really is.

"I use 'socialization' in the same sense as Scott did in his epic nearly twenty-something years of research set out in Genetics and the Social Behavior of the Dog by John Paul Scott and John Fuller. Socialization is a learning process. Though it takes place and is completed in a relatively brief period early in an animal's life, it acts to direct behaviors which develop later, mostly after sexual maturity.

"During this process of socialization, animals learn their species' specific language, be it a vocal language, body language or combination of both. They learn in an immature way their own species' specific social behaviors, which can then be expressed correctly in an adult form when the particular applicable situation occurs later in life. 'Socialization' is performing adult behaviors in a play fashion where a puppy learns it is a dog and not a person; where it learns the language and how to interact socially with dogs. An animal deprived of normal socialization in interactions with its parent(s) and sibs rarely fits in with its own species. It doesn't know how to interact socially or what the signals mean. It doesn't understand the language, be it body signals or vocal.

"Primary socialization is dog on dogs. The breeder plays no role except to let the litter stay together to at least ten weeks. People are not necessary for this socialization process in dogs. And in the strict sense, primary socialization of dogs on people does not occur.

"A secondary sort of socialization occurs during the same time period between 3 and 12 weeks of age but differs in that pups learn to interact something like socially with people, which appears to be interspecific socialization. Secondary socialization is unique to dogs, in that it allows dogs to interact socially, to some degree at least with a different species, people. It is really associative learning which only can occur in dogs before fear develops, starting late in the sixth week and escalating rapidly to the tenth week when it is maxed out. The touch, smell, sight of people is associated with only good stuff – low anxiety – because fear does not really start escalating until the seventh week. So the secondary socialization mostly takes place from birth to the end of the sixth week. Then, starting after pups are 12 weeks old, for the rest of their lives every social interaction as juveniles and adults, with dogs and with people, has a basis in what happened during the first 12 weeks. The breeder plays a role in the secondary socialization in that it is his/ her responsibility to expose the pups to humans during the critical time period.

"Therefore by stretching the definition of 'socialization' but not too far out of shape, we can call this "secondary socialization" because the dog does form at least some social relationships with people and the process does happen only during a short period early in the animal's life. No matter how much dog-people socialization takes place, dogs do not know people language except what they have acquired through associative learning. And people must learn their dog the same way. The communication systems are species-specific."

My statements regarding myths and facts are in regular type; Dr. Bailey's are in italics.

Myth --

You can't socialize your puppy until he's had all his shots. *Here socialize means exposure to anything.*

You can socialize your puppy to a crate. *Here socialize means habituate.*

Behavior modification is socialization. *Myth – see* Fact *below.*

You can't stress your puppy during socialization. *This is definitely a myth.*

Fact --

Puppies' primary socialization is to other dogs; secondary socialization is to another species -- humans *(cats, birds, etc.) only if exposed to them prior to fear development as per definition.*

Puppies need to become familiar with
their environment.

So, what does all this mean? It means that no one has a clear definition of terms, and "socialization" can mean what you think it means. Socialization means different things to different people, and the definition has been warped in the retelling. In fact, **Mat Ward** and **Catherine Bell** of the Association of Pet Behaviour Counsellors of Great Britain address this conundrum in their article "Are We Habituating to Inaccurate Terminology within the Field of Equestrian Science, and is this Overshadowing Our Progress?" http://tinyurl.com/ovgl8vv make this statement [They are talking about horses, but the principle is the same.]:

> "While it is exciting that the principles of learning theory are finally trickling through into professional horse training circles, there are still discrepancies between the ways certain learning theory terms are used and their well-established definitions. Without clarity within academic circles regarding terms relating to associative and non-associative learning processes, and the practical application of these processes, we risk retarding an opportunity to bring about meaningful training and welfare improvements in the wider equestrian world."

This is my speaking now – "socializing" is animal to animal, two living beings. However, in the realm of dogdom, the terms "socializing" and "habituating" have been lumped together under the term "socialization" for such a long time that it's difficult for many of us to separate them now – we are using the terms colloquially even though our use is technically incorrect. I think where the overlap stemmed from is that Scott and Fuller said that three to twelve weeks is a critical socialization period. They were talking about dogs. Later research was done on whether habituation to the environment needed to occur during the same period. In several subsequent articles by many authors, both the terms of "socialization" and "habituation" were used separately. At some point, the terms seemed to have morphed together so that "socialization" included habituation (which is another term having several meanings depending on the source; but for our purposes here, it means getting used to something).

In this book, I'm trying to marry the technical with the colloquial and talking about **a puppy's being comfortable around anything new before he is 16 weeks old** – including humans, other animals, and the sights, smells, sounds, and locations of everyday life – and, yes, that does lump together "socialization" and "habituating," but I talk about them separately. The process can be active or passive – active is what we do to help him along such as giving him a variety of chew toys and environmental enrichment, and passive is what he does himself such as chewing a leaf that he finds on the ground.

It's how a puppy:

- recognizes and interacts with the people and other animals he is living with
- develops the communication skills
- becomes accustomed to his environment, even the things in the environment he has never seen, heard, or smelled before
- learns to ignore nonthreatening things in the environment

To further muddy the waters, **many people confuse "socialization" with "behavior modification." The time for socialization is when the introduction** such as hearing thunder, meeting another dog, seeing a person with a beard, etc. **happens while he is a puppy with emphasis on before**

the onset of the fear period. Behavior modification is his learning to adapt after this time. Can a puppy learn after 16 weeks? Of course – and we'll talk about the best way to do it. However, these introductions, if done correctly, are MUCH easier before 16 weeks than behavior modification afterwards because we are working on a clean slate and takes much less time.

A Very Brief Background on Puppies and Socialization

John Paul Scott and **John L. Fuller**, in their 13-year study beginning in the 1950s at Bar Harbor, Maine, summarized in the classic book Genetics and the Social Behavior of the Dog (1965), set out to answer the question of what influence, if any, heredity had on behavior. Although they wanted to understand human behavior, they said, "Anyone who wishes to understand a human behavior trait or hereditary disease can usually find the corresponding condition in dogs with very little effort."

The book is fascinating – and a surprisingly easy read for me, a lay person. Without going into much detail here, one of their discoveries was that there were certain periods in a puppy's early life where certain events must take place, for example, contact with humans or exposure to other dogs. If those events did not take place, then that opportunity was lost, and the puppy would not develop to its fullest potential. Those periods were called "critical periods." For the most part, Scott and Fuller's work is the gold standard today on puppy developmental periods, with very little modification from their findings. Some of what they labeled as "critical" has been changed to "sensitive," meaning that the event does not have to take place exactly on X-day but may occur during a range of days.

Clarence Pfaffenberger worked with the Guide Dogs for The Blind and later worked with Scott and Fuller. His book The New Knowledge of Dog Behavior (1963) chronicles his research on how to find the ideal guide dog puppy. He applied their work to his own and came up with additional findings.

In the 1960s, the US Army was trying to breed a dog that was genetically and behaviorally sound for use in the military. It was called The Bio-Sensor Project" but was later changed to "Superdog." **Dr. Michael W. Fox** was involved in this project and has graciously given me a bit of insight and background into the project.

"While I was associate professor of psychology at Washington University, and having my PhD dissertation 'Integrative Development of Brain and Behavior in the Dog' published by the University of Chicago press and soon after the popular best selling version 'Understanding Your Dog' came out, the U.S. Army Veterinary Corps contacted me as a civilian advisor to improve the in-field performance and well-being of their military dogs serving in Viet Nam and being raised and trained at the Aberdeen Proving Grounds in Maryland.

"Based in part on procedures and findings detailed in my dissertation and summarized in 'Understanding Your Dog' [1972] (now available as an e-book on my website www.drfoxvet.com) I worked with Col Castleberry DVM and his staff to set up what we decided to call the Superdog Project. One officer, Jeff Lynn DVM, worked closely with me and earned a Masters degree from Washington University, Dept. of Psychology, detailing and evaluating this project, which was indeed a success.......

"So long as the American forces continue to operate in foreign countries with military dogs I would like to see better protective footwear and protective vests (including cooling vests) and goggles provided as needed for the dogs, and suitable local dogs, better adapted climate and disease-wise, being trained for military use and then brought back to the U.S. after service for adoption."

In Understanding Your Dog, Dr. Fox talks about "how environmental influences early in life can have profound and enduring effects on behavior."

"My own work with beagles exposed to thirty minutes of daily stimulation from birth until five weeks of age produced some very promising results but also revealed that extreme caution is necessary in order to avoid excessive stress and possible pathophysiological reactions.

Stimulation consisted of administering a wide variety of stimuli, such as brief cold exposure, cutaneous stimulation by stroking, stimulation of the balancing organs of the nervous system (the semicircular canals) by gently tilting and rotating the pup and stimulation of the visual and auditory systems by electronic flashes and clicks."

Dr. Carmen Battaglia, although not a participant in the Bio-Sensor project, came up with a series of handling exercises based on Dr. Fox's work which he now calls "Developing High Achievers," formerly known as "Early Neurological Stimulation." Dr. Battaglia says:

"Their studies [speaking of the Army's studies] confirmed that there are specific time periods early in life when neurological stimulation has optimum results. The first period involves a window of time that begins at the third day of life and lasts until the sixteenth day. It is believed that because this interval of time is a period of rapid neurological growth and development, and therefore is of great importance to the individual."

He came up with a series of five exercises (which appear in Appendix 1 in this book):

- Tactical stimulation (between toes)
- Head held erect
- Head pointed down
- Supine position
- Thermal stimulation

If these exercises are done correctly, puppies generally are more behaviorally sound than if they are not done, and they seem to have a beneficial effect on the puppy's mental and emotional development although there have not been any scientific tests to prove this. Dr. Battaglia says:

"Finally it seems clear that stress early in life can produce beneficial results. The danger seems to be in not knowing where the thresholds are for over and under stimulation. However, the absence or the lack of adequate amounts of stimulation generally will produce negative and undesirable results. Based on the above it is fair to say that the performance of most individuals can be improved including the techniques described above. Each contributes in a cumulative way and supports the next stage of development."

The next development in puppy socialization came from Dr. Ian Dunbar who both researched puppies and popularized what are now commonplace – puppy classes. These classes help puppies learn about playing and dog body language, BUT they are not a free-for-all where puppies can run around and do whatever they want.

Why are socialization and habituation important?

When a puppy is born, he does not know that he is a dog. He must learn through the process we call primary socialization. He must also learn how to interact with humans and other animals (secondary socialization) and also to be comfortable in his environment (habituation).

There are certain periods in a dog's life which are sensitive periods, during which a little learning goes a long way, and that learning influences his future behavior with both beneficial and damaging effects. We are concentrating on that learning here.

A dog's ultimate temperament is determined by his genes and how he is raised. Breeders can control whether they want temperament to be a part of their breeding program. How both breeders and owners raise the puppies for the first 16 weeks of their lives has a tremendous influence on whether the puppies will become well-adjusted and behaviorally fit adult dogs because puppies are, essentially, a clean slate. The small amounts of time in giving puppies positive early learning experiences will influence and will have a dramatic impact later in his life.

The influencers on how puppies act as adults are:

- The temperament of the dam/mother
- How the dam acts towards people, events, and other dogs
- How people interact with the puppy
- The age at which the puppy is separated from its mother and littermates – if he's separated too early, the puppy does not learn
  - o Dog body language and how to interpret it
  - o How to inhibit his bite
  - o Dog hierarchy
  - o When to tone down playing
- How many people, places, events, sounds, sights, and locations the puppy has been introduced to before 16 weeks.

More specifically, if a puppy does not have proper socialization and habituation, it will never reach its potential and will likely be:

- Shy or timid
- Fearful of anything new, both people and events
- Aggressive
- Unable to relate or communicate with other dogs
- Medically unsound (Since he is in a state of stress and anxiety, his body will not have the energy to fight off illnesses)

Proper socialization and habituation:

- Aids in depth perception

- Aids in learning to overcome frustration by teaching a puppy to develop self control and cope with problems rather than reacting fearfully or aggressively.

- Aids in problem solving

- Increases balance and body awareness

- Increases the connections between brain cells to provide a solid foundation to draw from when encountering new experiences

- Reduces
  o Aggression
  o Fights
  o Uncivilized behavior
  o Chasing animals
  o Extreme reactions
  o Anxiety. If a puppy is comfortable with everyday parts of his environment, then he does not waste energy by being fearful or anxious, and long-term anxiety can lead to a higher incidence of illnesses.

What we teach our puppies now doesn't always show up immediately but simmers around for months. It's not a knee-jerk reaction. It's the basis for social skills of confidence, behavioral stability, and self assurance. We need to recognize and avoid stressors in our puppies early on so those stressors don't affect our dogs later in life.

To sum up, the term "socialization" has different definitions depending on who is using it. In this book, we are talking about a puppy's being comfortable around anything new before he is 16 weeks old and includes

- Primary socialization of dogs with dogs

- Secondary socialization of dogs with humans (and other animals)
- Habituation to things and events in the environment

It can be passive where the puppy discovers things on his own or active where we help him.

Because you are reading this book, you likely already know about this, so I'm not going to dwell on it other than to say that we have control over many of these factors! Let's make good use of it.

Chapter 2

A Brief Look at
Puppy Developmental Periods

What is a Sensitive Period, and what does this mean to you and your puppy?

A **Sensitive Period** is a time during which the puppy undergoes dramatic behavior changes and forms habits which stay with him pretty much for the rest of his life – a little goes a long way. A habit is easier to form than to break. If he is introduced to a vacuum cleaner, for example, during this critical period, he can either be afraid of it or he can accept it. What the puppy will do depends a lot on how it was introduced and his perception based on our reaction to the situation.

While he may be startled initially, what happens afterwards is what's important. If a puppy is scared, we want to comfort him so we try to soothe him by making a fuss and talking to him in a high-pitched voice – and we also have a very concerned look on our faces. Our puppy could easily perceive that voice and look as meaning, "Boy, that vacuum cleaner is something terrible." On the other hand, if we act nonchalant and tell him how silly he is and give him a treat for looking at us, what lesson have we taught? That if he is frightened, to turn to us for guidance. If we aren't scared, why should he be?

Think of how different a baby is raised in Alaska, New York City, and the jungles of South America. What would happen if an Alaskan baby were magically transported to South America when he was three months old? She would probably act basically the same because she does not have enough life experiences yet. Would she behave differently if she moved when she was six years old? Now she has more experience and would have to unlearn, relearn, and learn new things. How about 15 years old? An even bigger challenge because there is more to overcome. That's the nature vs. nurture debate – how our behavior is affected by both our genes and our upbringing.

Our dogs have just about all the brain cells they are going to have by the time they are four weeks old. What they don't have is the connections between the cells, and that's what socialization and habituation are all about – making those connections. The more connections they have, the more solid the foundation is for the rest of their lives.

The changes do not even need to be drastic to be profound. Those connections can come after the sensitive period, but they likely will not have the long-lasting effects.

> **True story** – Human equivalent – after I graduated from college, I went to Europe for the summer. I was bombarded every day with new places, new customs, new relationships, new problems to solve. I came back home a *very* different person, but my family was virtually the same as when I left. It was difficult for me to adjust because I had grown at an exponential rate because of all of those experiences crammed into those ten weeks, but my family had grown at a much slower rate. There were other people on the trip who couldn't take the drastic changes and came back to the States before the end of summer. There were others who chose to stay in Europe and did not come

back at all. All of our experiences – and outcomes – were very, very different. Did I acclimate back to what I was before? Of course. Was I the same person I was before I left? Not really.

One final note about developmental periods. It was previously thought that the best time for a puppy to be adopted by his new family is seven weeks or 49 days. Many sources agree that the earliest that puppies should leave the nest is eight weeks, and ten weeks is even better (provided that the breeder has done proper socialization, environmental enrichment, and habituation) because up to ten weeks, the puppies are learning about other dogs and how to develop good social skills from their littermates and mom.

Very, very, very briefly, puppy developmental periods are approximately as follows. These are not exact times because dog size and the purpose dogs were bred for differ.

Birth – 2 weeks The Neonatal Period

The new puppy has only the senses of smell, taste, and touch. He eats, sleeps, stumbles around, pees, and poops during this period, and that's pretty much it.

2-3 Weeks – The Transitional Period

During this period, the puppy's eyes and ears open and he begins to walk rather than crawl. He also becomes aware of his littermates and his environment. He begins to become a dog.

3-13 Weeks – The Socialization Period

This is the optimal socialization time for a puppy where he is like a sponge when his senses are developing and refining. His motor skills are improving. He is making associations with other living beings and his environment. His brain is changing so that events he encounters during this time will likely have lifelong consequences.

13 weeks – 6 months – Adolescence

The behavior patterns that the puppy has developed begin to mature, hormones kick in, and puppies begin to test boundaries. That sweet little puppy that you brought home where you were the center of his world has now changed into – (gasp!) – a teenager. Now there is a conflict between what he has learned previously (boring) and what he is learning now (exciting). He seems to act like an adult one minute and a puppy the next. The larger the breed, the longer the adolescent period. With the giant breeds, adolescence can last until he is three years old.

6 months on – Adulthood

By this time, your puppy has sorted out his world. He has definite opinions about the way things should be, and he is on his way to becoming an adult.   Much of his behavior is ingrained.

Interspersed with these periods are fear periods, the first being approximately 7-11 weeks and the second 6-14 months. The fear periods are important developmentally and harken back to before dogs became domesticated and they were wolves. Puppies had to learn what is safe and what is dangerous so they would not be harmed by predators. During these fear periods, your puppy can become a different dog because yesterday nothing bothered him, and today he seems afraid of everyday objects and events. (We talk more about fear and helping your puppy to overcome fear in Appendix 6.)

BREEDER'S SECTION

Chapter 3

Timeline for the Breeder

Note: References to the "breeder"
include the breeder and the breeder's
family and to "people" are to people
other than the breeder and the breeder's
family.

The focus of this book is not on the care of the litter per se but on how to aid in its behavioral development. There are many other sources that address caring for the litter that I suggest you consult if you are a breeder or thinking about becoming one.

I am assuming that the breeder has researched and chosen breeding stock carefully and has taken care of the dam by providing good veterinary care and nutrition. Because the puppies receive chemical signals through the placenta during gestation, the breeder should also keep her as stress-free as possible since the more stable the mom is, the more stable the puppies are. Research has shown that if the breeder talks to, plays with, and pets the mom during pregnancy, the pups benefit from that, as well. If she is kept outdoors in a kennel, there is less likelihood that the human/dog interaction takes place, so it's best to keep mom inside the house and yet another reason not to purchase a puppy from a pet store, most of which get their puppies from puppy mills.

Keeping in mind that socialization is dog to dog and then dog to people, the bulk of what people do as breeders and owners is habituation and environmental enrichment. What I am suggesting here is a range of possibilities in an orderly manner based on research and specific breeder suggestions. I have spoken to and/or done research on pet breeders, show breeders, and sport breeders. They generally have similar information, but the timing of introduction of the various exercises and objects differs because each puppy is different due to differences in development after birth neurologically, physiologically, and physically because of the timing of when the eggs were fertilized in the womb was different and other factors.

Socialization, habituation, and environmental enrichment are extremely important for singleton or two-puppy litters, especially after the third week because the puppies simply don't have the range of play and other experiences as they would in a larger litter. If you cannot find other puppies for yours to play with, ask another breeder to rub some towels over her puppies to capture the smell. Rub that towel on your puppy's bedding and toys, and do your best to imitate play with another puppy.

I have included the earliest times to introduce experiences, but please adapt them to your puppies – one puppy may be ready on Day X while another is not until a week later. These are not hard-and-fast rules. (Read "Why Not Seven Weeks--The Forty-Ninth Day Revisited" by **Dr. Ed Bailey** http://tinyurl.com/o4zp2vq which discusses why all puppies may be the same age chronologically but not developmentally.)

Kristin Hotti http://GoldenGateLabradoodles.com concurs. Her comments are:

> "There really are not specifics that relate to 'Week X' or 'Week Y.' For my breed, in almost all cases the 'schedule' you suggest is off, sometimes by as much as 2 weeks. All breeds AND litters are different. Breeders need to observe their puppies carefully from litter to litter to determine what is development-appropriate.

> "I have puppy litters scarfing down puppy mush at 3.5 weeks and others who refuse anything except from mama til 5 weeks. Eyes open from 12-18 days. We don't take our puppies outside for more than a minute or two until about 5 weeks. I have added many comments about my own experiences with my 23 litters. Perhaps it would be more meaningful to list the ideas as 'when appropriate' or stipulating 'typically between 2 and 4 weeks.' Otherwise, you risk a breeder reading the first few weeks breakdown and dismissing it all as not applicable."

There are several suggestions for each week, but it is not an exhaustive list. It is critical to do the first two weeks' exercises exactly as Dr. Battaglia suggests on a daily basis. Hopefully, every breeder can do the Week 3 and following exercises daily. If all the exercises cannot be done to every puppy every day after the first two weeks, then do as many as possible and rotate them so that you cover them all.

The specific active exercises should be brief, no longer than one minute in the beginning and increasing in length – and done with each puppy singly unless otherwise noted. There may be several sessions per day, but again, start with just two sessions, and then increase the time and frequency as the puppies' attention spans get a little longer.

Weeks 3 to 6 are the most important times for the breeder to introduce her puppies to the human world, but both she and the new owner should continue for many months thereafter. Puppies who are "pre-stressed" (meaning that they receive exposure to events and sensory experiences before fear develops) and those that receive further stimulation until 12-16 weeks are behaviorally sounder and more stable or fit than those who do not. Introduce the stressors as systematically as possible where the breeder and owner can control the puppy's experience.

Environmental enrichment items that the breeder and then owner introduce offer both physical and mental tests that challenge the puppy and expose him to novel encounters that help him cope in later life. There are generally five categories of enrichment:

- Food (feeding different foods in different receptacles)
- Novelty (changing or moving the whelping pen, introducing items into the whelping area, and taking the puppy on excursions out of the whelping area)
- Sensory (smell, hearing, touch, taste, sight)
- Social (contact with other dogs, humans, and other animal species)
- Training

Please be sure to look at Appendix 2 because there are some wonderful photographs illustrating many of the concepts introduced here.

Week 1

The puppies' eyes and ears are not opened yet, so their only senses are touch, taste, and smell. They are completely dependent on their mother and sleep most of the time. When they are awake, they can crawl, eat, and pee, and poop – but they need mom to stimulate them.

From Day 3 on, you need to ensure that any associations the puppy has are positive. Also during this period handle and talk to the puppies daily. There should not be any visitors during this week.

Smell

Hold the puppy against your chest so he can smell you and hear your heart beat.

Touch

Do the Early Neurological Stimulation exercises. Because Dr. Battaglia has requested that his article be published in toto, it is included as Appendix 1. Please refer to that now.

Location and Surface

Move puppies to another blanket.

The Bare Essentials

Do the Early Neurological Stimulation exercises.

Week 2

The eyes and ears open towards the end of this period, so the puppies can now see and hear.

Smell

Hold the puppy against your chest so he can smell you.

Sound

- Hold the puppy against your chest so he can hear your heartbeat.
- Play classical music at a low volume.
- Play television at a low volume.

Touch

Continue with Early Neurological Stimulation exercises (See Appendix 1).

Location and Surface

Move puppies to another blanket.

The Bare Essentials

Early Neurological Stimulation.

Week 3

Now that puppies can see and hear, they begin to play with each other and learn about their surroundings. They begin to learn about how to be a dog. THIS is socializing!

This week is when environmental enrichment is important because you are taking advantage of the puppies' newfound senses without any fear being attached to it since the fear response has not developed yet. They also can walk – or are feebly attempting to walk and are learning to balance.

Now is a good time to introduce a variety of sounds. The puppy may try to see where the sound is coming from or may startle, but the breeder should not intervene at this point because the puppy will look for the origin of the sound and then go back to what he was doing. If the breeder makes a fuss, then the response to the next loud sound may be exaggerated.

(As a side note, for a long, long, long time in the dog training field, we were taught to ignore any fear responses in older dogs because we would be "reinforcing" the fear if we paid attention to it. Perhaps this is where that myth began. Because the fear response *is* developed in older dogs – most notably beginning at five weeks, peaking seven, and then beginning again at four months – we *do* need to respond by desensitizing them to whatever they are afraid of.)

Sight

- Put plastic bottles and a few toys of different shapes and sizes in the whelping box away from the sleeping area. These toys should have different shapes, colors, and textures, and be sure that the puppies cannot swallow them or any part of them.
  - o Fabric
  - o PVC pipe in 6-12 inch lengths
  - o Rubber
  - o Small plastic brown vitamin or pill bottles with the lids removed
  - o Squeaky toys
- Drag a toy or cloth from puppies both inside and outside the box so the puppies can see movement.
- Hang a mobile above whelping box for several minutes every day.
- Change the light levels by turning one and then several lights on and off.

Smell

- Introduce new smells – herbs, flowers – by placing these in the nest room.

- Use towels to introduce other scents – and this takes a bit of preparation before birth. You know that your puppies will be visiting a veterinarian's office. Ask your vet to hang a towel in his office to absorb the smells for about a week. Then hang that towel in your puppy area. You can also use towels to soak up odors from other venues such as beaches, city streets, wooded areas, fields, etc. Replace them and/or introduce new scents on a weekly basis.

- Start nose work by putting meat-based baby food or puree on your fingers (no onion powder, please!) and lure him around the pen.

- Put a treat on the ground a short distance from the puppy so he will move toward it and find it. Advance by putting the treat further away, and then out of sight.

Sound

Note: Make sure the puppy gets to hear as many sounds as possible. Introduce different noises starting with the puppies hearing them in a group and then individually. Play these sounds at various times throughout the day for one to two minutes at a time, including while they are eating.

Introduce sudden sounds (such as pots and pans or hammering) – try not to let the puppies see you as the source of the noise. Introduce the noises first when the puppies are all together and then when they are separated from their littermates. They might startle briefly but then return to their previous activity. Again, ignore their reaction because fear has not yet developed.

Many of the items that are discussed here and throughout the rest of the book are available on one of my websites, www.DogBooksLibrary.com, which is an Amazon-affiliate and a Dogwise-affiliate site, meaning you may purchase anything on the site at the same price as Amazon or Dogwise. I have handpicked the products and books found there. There are only items relevant to each particular category, unlike Amazon where you search for one item and unrelated products pop up.

- Drop pots and pans and their lids on the floor.
- Drop your car keys.
- Use a hammer.
- **If you live in a rural setting, it is imperative that the puppies are exposed to city noises**. There are CDs with a variety of different noises including fireworks and thunder. Play them at various times during the day for a few minutes. The volume does not have to be loud, but play them several times a day. Puppies can tell the difference between tape recordings and the real thing, but this introduces them to a variety of noises to which they likely will need to become accustomed.
- Open and close (slam) doors, including the refrigerator door and cabinet doors.
- Open and close the garage door.
- Play the radio on various stations.
- Put pennies in a small plastic bottle and softly shake.
- Ring doorbells.
- Shake a metal cookie tray.
- Toss things such as a plastic bottle with a few coins in it near the whelping box while puppies are awake and also while asleep.
- Turn on the
  - o Blender
  - o Dishwasher

o   Garbage disposal

o   Hair dryer

o   Rug shampooer

o   Trash compacter

o   Vacuum cleaner

Touch

- Touch and rub your hand all over the puppy's body, making sure you touch in the direction of hair growth using a

  o   Plastic brush

  o   Rubber glove

  o   Sheepskin

  o   Towel

  o   Woolen glove

- Examine your puppy as a vet would examine a dog – Check teeth, eyes, ears, and nose.

- Handle and gently squeeze each toe separately.

- Put your fingers between the pads of the feet.

- Gently pinch his skin to simulate how a puppy vaccine feels.

Challenges and Coping Skills

- You can guide him over a low elevated object by putting meat-based baby food on your fingers. Make sure it does not contain onion or onion powder.

- Each puppy should be removed from the rest of the litter for a few minutes per day, at first with another puppy and then by himself, so he will learn to be alone and also to prepare him for the time when he goes to his new home. Take him into other rooms in the house or hold him on your lap while sitting in a chair or on the floor, or lying on the sofa. Play with the puppy in the beginning, and then give him some toys to play with so he learns he can amuse himself. Try to repeat this separation daily until the puppies go to their new home.

Learning and Training

Begin potty training by sectioning off the nest into three areas – one is a sleeping area; one is a playing area; one is a potty area, each having a different surface – for example, if the sleeping area is carpet, introduce a grass surface for the potty area to help the puppies choose a potty area other than the nest area. (Fresh Patch or sod is perfect for this.)

If you go to here http://www.freshpatch.com/wolff, then you can get your first delivery for only $10 including shipping and then order additional units as you need them on Amazon here http://www.dogbookslibrary.com/potty-training-or-housetraining.php#Products.

Location or Surface

- Move the whelping box to a different location.
- Walking on different surfaces daily such as
   o Bubble wrap

o Cement floor

o Crumpled paper

o Dry bathtub

o Grass, both dry and wet

o Gravel

o Linoleum

o Rocks

o Rubber mat

o Rug samples of different textures – indoor/outdoor, shag, tufted, sisal, etc.

o Tarp

o Tile

o Window screen

o Wood floor or deck

o Wood shavings or chips

Also look at the **Checklist for Owners** for other suggestions of surfaces.

The Bare Essentials

- Gently pick up each puppy daily and stroke and examine him.

- Separate each puppy from the litter for short periods.

- Introduce him to new sights and sounds.

Week 4

Teeth are coming in and puppies are being weaned, meaning that mom is not too happy about nursing (it hurts!) and makes herself less available.

Puppies are socializing with their littermates and learning

- How to communicate
- How to inhibit their bites during play
- More about the world outside the whelping box
- About social hierarchy
- ...as well as becoming more physically coordinated.

Food and feeding

- Put a barrier in front of the food bowls, so the puppies have to figure out how to get around it, which, at the same time, teaches them to deal with frustration.
- Touch while eating.
- Feed good quality solid food.
- Add treats into the food bowl while the puppy is eating.

Smell

- Put different scents in a plate near the whelping box.
  - o Animal (synthetic scents can be purchased at sporting goods stores.)
  - o Cooking extracts such as vanilla, anise, lemon, etc.
  - o Herbs
  - o Spices
- Open a window (weather permitting) so the puppies can smell the outdoors.

Sound

Play a different station on the radio every day – everything from country to rock to classical.

Touch

Teach each puppy to accept being restrained. Hold him gently by putting him between your legs and linking your hands around his chest. He should wiggle and try to get free. Only let him go when he calms down. At first let him go immediately, and then increase the time he needs to be calm.

Use Ttouch circular motions around the mouth area. (See the Bibliography for Ttouch or Tellington Touch.)

Challenges and Coping Skills

- Introduce more shapes and textures of toys and other objects – such as boxes or agility obstacles scaled to size, that the puppies can:
  o Carry
  o Climb on
  o Go through
  o Move around
  o Pull
  o Share/tug with littermates
  o Cut holes in cardboard boxes (some right side up and some upside down) and put toys and food inside so the puppies can crawl to go inside them.
  o Turn buckets on their sides and put toys inside so puppies get used to movement under their feet.
  o Hide a toy or treat under a cloth or box cover to make the puppy search for it, building his self esteem and confidence.
  Refer to Appendix 2 for photos of how one breeder sets up her puppy living area.
- Introduce something new daily both with new objects and by moving the obstacles and toys to different areas. You can make changes by simply changing the location of the obstacles. "The Puppy Headstart Program" by **Corally**

Burmaster at The Clicker Training Center has some excellent photos of how to set up and change obstacles and equipment.

Learning and Training

- While each puppy is away from the nest, start doing some simple training exercises such as luring them into a Sit.

- Begin to teach the Recall by calling the puppy, moving away from him, so he sees and follows your moving, and then give him a treat when he comes to you.

- Have the puppy chase a toy by rolling it on the ground or moving it erratically.

Location and Surface

- When the puppies are together, they play with each other and toys while becoming confident around each other. Take each puppy from the nest area for longer periods of time and bring a few toys along so he not only has something to play with, but playing with those same toys helps in developing independence.

- Take him/them outdoors if it is warm enough. You can put him in an Xpen, but be sure to stay to supervise.

- Guide or lure him under a chair and between the legs.

Visitors

New visitors, both men and women, should sit on the floor, so the puppies can approach them at their own pace. Each person can pick up, hold, and talk to each puppy and touch them all over their bodies. (Be sure that the visitors have washed their hands and removed their shoes first. You can provide them with disposable foot coverings.)

Show visitors how to pick up the puppies so you do not hurt or scare them because you want the puppies to feel secure and to trust people. Most people pick up puppies similar to the way they pick up a baby, and that is incorrect because puppies have a different type of joint than we do, and picking a puppy up the same way we pick up a baby can hurt and even injure them. Instruct the visitors to:

- Get behind the puppy.
- Put both hands under the rib cage right behind the front legs.
- Pick up the chest first with both hands and then immediately slide one hand to support his rear end and back legs. Don't let the legs dangle! (Some people like to put the palm underneath supporting the chest and their index and middle finger between the legs to support the front of the ribs.)
- As you move your hand to the rear, bring the puppy towards your chest.
- Support his body by placing your arm underneath. (Cradle him like you would a baby, but don't pick him up as you would pick up a baby.)
- Keep supporting his rear while you hold him – for heaven's sake, don't drop him!
- When you put him down, be sure all his feet are planted on the floor before you let go.

Children should be seated on the floor, and you place the puppy in their lap. Tell children to remain seated and gently pet the puppy from the head to the tail. Don't allow toddlers to hold the puppy because they do not have enough coordination themselves. Never leave a child alone with a puppy and don't take your eyes off them even for a split second.

Puppies can also lick some pureed meat off the tip of visitor's fingers, so they equate humans with good stuff. The most fun for visitors is engaging the puppies by playing with toys. Use soft toys that the puppy can carry but which are too big to be swallowed.

The Bare Essentials

- Remove each puppy separately daily.
- Increase the time the puppies spend away from the litter and time they spend with people.
- Place new smells and novel objects in the puppy area daily.
- Begin "challenge" training, potty training, along with puppy-geared obedience training.
- Let each puppy be exposed to new environments.
- Give the puppies items to chew.
- Let each puppy meet new people.

Week 5

During this time, puppies are learning bite inhibition and communication skills between littermates.

Food and Feeding

- Begin feeding away from mom and the litter.
- Begin feeding him from your hand. (You can use his food as treats in training.)
- Use different bowls for feeding and move the feeding dish to different locations. Bowls can be
  - o Ceramic
  - o Foil trays
  - o Frying pans

- o Pans
- o Paper
- o Pie plates
- o Steel
- o Wobbly
- Feed in different areas
  - o In a crate with the door open and then closed near the puppy pen
  - o In a crate with the door open and then closed away from the puppy pen
  - o In a gated-off room
  - o In the car
  - o On the front porch
  - o On the landing to stairs (Secure the area so he cannot fall down the stairs.)

Sight
- Open an ironing board.
- Let him see and then hear the vacuum cleaner.
- Let him see kid's toys that move around on wheels.

Smell
- Introduce the smell of the new owners by putting t-shirts or towels with each owner's scent inside that puppy's crate. Put toys and treats inside the plastic crate and leave the doors off so each puppy can explore his new owner's smell and associate it with good stuff.
- Bring items from outside inside
  - o Mowed grass
  - o Leaves and branches from nonpoisonous trees
  - o Flowers

o Earth

o Rocks

Sound

- Continue sound conditioning.
- Play video games.
- Snap open a plastic bag.

Touch

- Begin grooming with a comb or brush that has plastic bristles, not a wire slicker brush because those are too sharp for his delicate skin.
- Restrain him gently on his side. He will likely squirm, but wait until he relaxes to release him.

Challenges and Coping Skills

- Put increasingly difficult toys in the puppy area including
  o Boxes with doors cut out so they can go in and out of them
  o Boxes, wicker baskets, or other baskets that they can climb in or out of
  o Plastic bottles with rocks that make noise when they roll
  o Suspended Kongs or tennis balls
  o Things that wobble (Buy a balance board or make your own.)
  o Trays with rocks and/or water to get them used to having their feet wet to prepare them to potty outside
  o Tunnels (Purchase one or make a tunnel from chairs and bed sheets. Move it to different locations.)
- If weather permits, take them outdoors and use the misting setting on the hose to prepare them for rain.

- Put a collar on while they are eating, playing with littermates or toys, or doing something else, so they are not thinking about this darned thing around their necks.

- Put a small step by stacking books or boards and/or a ramp in the entrance of the whelping area so they learn to go up and down to get in and out.

- Put plastic crates (take off the doors) and half crates in the whelping area so the puppies can climb over them and go in and out.

- Begin independence training where you leave each puppy by himself in his sleeping area during the day. Leave him some familiar toys to play with. At first, leave that area for short periods of time. Don't return if he is crying. Wait for him to be quiet. The next step is to sit in an adjacent room with the door open. Then close the door for short periods, again, not returning unless he is quiet. Finally, extend his alone time. This is a lot of work for you, but it will ease in the transition and help prevent separation anxiety in his new home.

Learning and Training

- Teach the puppies not to jump up when getting out of the pen. Only let them out when they are either standing or, preferably, sitting. This teaches him self control. First teach each puppy individually by approaching the pen, and when he jumps, turn away until you can open the pen and he does not jump. Then train another one individually until the entire litter is trained. Then work with two puppies at a time, then three, etc. until the entire litter sits when you approach. Repeat the exercise when another person accompanies you. (Anytime you change one element of training, it is a different exercise to your puppy, and he has to re-learn the exercise.)

- Introduce other animals. Make sure they are healthy and like to be around puppies!

Location and Surface

- Move the nest area to a different location.
- Take the puppies on a field trip in a safe area that other dogs do not frequent.
  - o School
  - o Parking lot
  - o Baseball or soccer field

People

- Introduce children and carefully supervise their interaction. Instruct the children how to handle the puppies – they must sit on the floor and stroke the puppy gently, or they can play fetch.
- Take the puppy to a playground so he can hear and see children running and screaming.
- Introduce each puppy to delivery people.

The Bare Essentials

- Continue with the Week 4 activities.
- Introduce other safe animals.
- Lengthen alone time from littermates.

Week 6

Take mom away from sleeping with the litter at night – you want to give her a break, too!

Sound

This is the last week for sound conditioning.

Touch

Begin Handling Exercises as described below and also in Appendix 8. This is a series of exercises designed for each puppy to become accustomed to being handled by a veterinarian and groomer.

- While you are at home, handle each puppy as a vet would during an exam. Choose a quiet place and time when the puppy is relaxed. **Give him treats during this whole process and verbal reassurance.** Go slowly, and let him become comfortable with each part of the process before proceeding to the next part.

- Several times a day, pick up each puppy and put him on a raised surface such a table, a countertop, your washer or dryer, or some other raised surface on top of which you have put a rubber mat so he will not be afraid of getting up on the examination or grooming table.

- Now get him ready for the examination in a vet's office.
  o Give him a bear hug while you are facing him for several seconds. He may struggle, so wait him out. The struggle should only last a few seconds. As soon as he relaxes, release him that very instant.
  o Then hug him from behind him and wait for relaxation.
  o Cradle him in your arms while letting his head rest in the crook of your arm.
  o Put him down and gently take each leg and pull it from his body, then push it close to his body.
  o Then move each leg up and down, and then in a circle. Be careful not to stretch too far because the puppy's joints are not the same as ours – we can easily move our arms and legs in a circle because they are a ball-and-socket joint and move in a circle, while the puppy's are similar to hinges that move up and down and back and forth and don't have the same range of motion.

o   To get him into position for x-ray procedures, put him on his right side and stretch his legs out away from you. Then do the same thing on his left side. Lay him on his back and give him a belly rub. Then gently stretch his legs out.

o   Then hold him on his side for a few seconds. Remember, you are doing this while he is relaxed. However, he may struggle a bit for a few seconds. Try it again, but this time give him treats the instant you put him on his side.

o   Touch all parts of his body. Scratch his tummy, under his chin, and behind his ears. Pet him with long, gentle strokes. Then start stroking him in a clockwise circular motion as if you are giving him an all-over body massage. Make sure it is clockwise. This is one of the Ttouch techniques.

o   As he gets comfortable with that, then touch his ears, look inside his ears, stroke his muzzle, open his mouth, touch his teeth and gums, move his tongue around. Pick up his paws. Run your hands down his legs. Gently squeeze his feet, toes, and tail. Hold and then squeeze gently his shoulders and then his hips between your hands. Press gently on his spine.

People

Take the puppies to the veterinarian for their first visit, but this visit should be an introductory, short, fun visit where the staff can ooh and aah over the puppies. The vet can examine them, but no vaccines or other procedures should be done at this time. The puppies are used to being handled by you while they are at home, so acclimate them to the same handling by you at the vet's and then by the staff by repeating the same handling exercises.

Challenges and Coping Skills

• Put the puppy in a wagon or stroller.

- Teach the puppy to ride in a crate in the car.

- Take the puppy outside at night – remember that his feet should not touch the ground, so either carry him or use one of the carriers discussed earlier.

- Weather permitting, take the puppies outside and turn on the sprinkler while they are playing. It helps prepare them for rain and also pottying on wet grass.

- Put the puppies in their individual crates to sleep in at night with their new owner's scent in each crate.

- Introduce motorized toys (This one is GoGoDogPals.)

Learning and Training

- Have the puppies come to you through a tunnel.

- Have them come to you by going over a small obstacle – set up books, PVC pipe, hula hoops on the ground, anything that moves when he walks on it – and give him a scrumptious treat when he gets to you.

- Begin to teach Sit. Be sure that you have a release command – I never use the word "okay" as a release because it is used frequently in everyday conversation. Puppies do not understand the context of our sentences and listen for sounds that they know. They only hear "blah, blah, blah" until they are taught to associate a specific sound (word) with a specific action.

True story – I know a very well-trained dog that was killed because his release command was "okay." The dog had been taught to wait at curbs until he was released. The owner was walking with her son and the dog, and they came to a particularly busy intersection where they waited and waited and waited. She turned to her son and said, "After this next car, it will be okay," and the dog stepped into the street because it heard "okay" and was killed. Please do not use "okay" as a release word.

Location and Surface

- Take them to an enclosed area that has fallen branches, large rocks, wet grass, piles of leaves and have them follow you or come to you. Hide behind trees and have them find you.
- Move the whelping box to a different location.

The Bare Essentials

- Continue with and intensify the previous week's exercises and activities.
- Take the puppies to the veterinarian.
- Have each puppy sleep away from the litter.

Week 7

Puppies should be completely weaned because now he has all his 28 baby teeth. Puppies are curious but cautious because this time is the beginning of the Fear Impact Period. Keep novelty to a minimum.

Puppies are really sponges at this age, and any experience they encounter at this age will have a lifelong impact. Be careful not to expose them to any stressors! We used to think that the seventh week was the optimum time for puppies to go to their new home, but that thinking has changed because of the valuable lessons puppies learn about doggie social behavior from their littermates and mom and also because it is very stressful to take them away from their litter at this time. If a puppy is shipped to his new home in a crate and has not been accustomed to it, then he may have a lifelong fear of confinement.

Food and Feeding

- Feed puppies singly away from the litter – no more communal feeding. Be sure to give them a lot of interactive toys so they can work to get their food from a toy rather than its being served in a bowl.
- Feed four meals a day.

Challenges and Coping Skills

- Put collars on while they are feeding to get them used to the feel of a collar around their neck while, at the same time, their minds are on something else.
- Puppies should spend less and less time with mom.

The Bare Essentials

Continue with and intensify the previous week's exercises and activities, especially doing some of the exercises at night outside.

Week 8

This week is a good time to start obedience training if you haven't already begun. Puppies have short attention spans, so each lesson should be no more than a minute.

Sound

Try to avoid loud noises at this point because of the Fear Impact Period.

Touch

Stay away from any rough handling, especially with children.

Learning and Training

Introduce the Come command in a new area because he is beginning to explore but still needs the comfort of knowing you are close. Take the puppy to a friend's house with an enclosed yard and where you know that the yard is safe – no pesticides and no escape routes. Let the puppy explore the yard. While he is exploring but not watching you, you hide, so he is now alone. When he notices you are gone, he will begin to cry. Let him cry for about ten seconds and then you magically appear and say "come." Pet him, and make a big fuss when he comes to you. Repeat a couple of times in the same location (if you can!) and then repeat in another location at another friend's house. You have just taught him that even if the world is way more interesting than you are, it's his job to keep track of you and check in. Suggest this exercise to his new owners.

Week 9

The Bare Essentials

- Continue with and intensify the previous week's exercises and activities.
- Train outdoors and train at night.

Week 10

The Bare Essentials

It's now time for the puppies to leave the nest permanently. When puppies go to their new home, the breeder should tell the new owners how much socialization the puppy has had and let them know what to do to continue socialization and exposure to new things – recommending this book is a perfect! (Shameless self promotion……..)

Chapter 4

Environmental Enrichment for Puppies

This article originally appeared in the June 1989 issue of the **AKC GAZETTE** and is reprinted with the permission of both the AKC Gazette and the authors, **Peter and Nancy Bickerton Vollmer.** Thank you so much!

Today's knowledgeable puppy raisers are talking about early stimulation and enrichment, bonding, socialisation and subordination - concepts stemming from the realm of animal behaviour research and being successfully applied to puppy rearing.

One particularly fun and exciting way to take advantage of the insights gleaned from animal research is to introduce very young puppies to obstacles. Working with puppy obstacles can prepare them for the challenges that await them as adults, whether they are in the show ring or climbing a motel stairway on a family vacation! A pup that can go through a soft cloth tunnel, splash gleefully in a shallow wading pool and scramble over a stack of newspapers when it is seven weeks old will be better prepared to attempt an agility course, a track laid in difficult terrain, the rough going of herding or hunting events or a backpacking trip in the Sierra Nevada wilderness. A stroll in the park or a turn around the confirmation ring should be as easy as digging in the yard.

Understanding Puppy Abilities

A major breakthrough in understanding how young, developing mammals are affected by their environment occurred in the 1940s. Dr. Donald Hebb, of McGill University, discovered that rats raised in homes as pets far out-performed the laboratory cage-reared group in their ability to solve maze problems.

Upon further testing, researchers found rats raised under even more stimulating conditions showed less fear when confronted with new experiences, matured faster, were more resistant to disease and were better problem solves as adults.

Since the 1940s, these findings have been confirmed by researchers studying other species, including dogs. In the 1960s, Dr. Michael Fox and his associates tested puppies and found that early stimulating experiences have similar positive effects on their development.

These discoveries, referred to as early enrichment, as well as the Bar Harbor discoveries of Drs. Fuller and Scott (see Gazette, June, July and August 1988) and the wild canine research of Dr. David Mech of Purdue University (see National Geographic, May, 1987) have given the dog fancy new insights into the wonderful, often scary, always complex task of bringing up that beloved, special puppy or long planned and eagerly awaited litter. On the down side, researchers found that if very young dogs were not quickly successful in solving test problems, they might give up and not try again. Sometimes a particular puppy would not only quit, but become highly emotional and begin crying, whining or howling.

Puppies which had a startling, frightening or painful experience while being tested could develop an aversion to the entire test situation and continue to act frightened when subsequently retested.

'The more you work with your pup, using safe and effective methods, the closer the bond will become.'

Achieving Success

Here's how breeders and new puppy owners can take advantage of the positive effects that early enrichment produces. To make sure all the pups have a worthwhile, positive experience when doing the enrichment exercises, it is important to follow these guidelines. Everyone will have more fun if you don't think of the exercises as tests, but as things you can do to help and encourage puppies to use their heads, while learning to overcome fears and apprehensions. In other words, don't ask the puppies to conquer the enrichment tasks on their own. Instead, give them the "answers" to the problems by using the right teaching techniques. As an example, a goal might be to teach a pup to walk through a ladder that is lying on the ground. Instead of starting at one end, and coaxing, pushing or dragging him all the way to the other, try placing his hind legs just inside the last rung and encouraging him to "go for it." In no time, your puppy will by running through the entire ladder as if he were at a football practice session.

Try not to drill puppies with endless repetitions. Be satisfied with little successes, and give them time to assimilate the tasks physically and mentally. A carefree, playful attitude on your part will carry over to the pup's attitude toward the tasks at hand and to you as the team leader.

Recommendations to Breeders

Amanda Gibson's Zephyr Puppy enrichment can begin with daily weighing, starting shortly after birth, and continue through three weeks. Before returning the neonates to mother, briefly rock each pup back and forth, and up and down. Rub the coat briskly with your hands, and gently finger the webbing between the toes. Rub the ears and muzzle, and then invert the pup so it is facing the ceiling, and again, rock back and forth, up and down.

This handling provides feedback to the central nervous system via the receptor pathways involved in reporting touch and balance, and, if done regularly and consistently, stimulates the developing nervous system. Shortly after their fourth week, the pups begin to explore their surroundings in earnest. At this time, puppy obstacles can be used to encourage problem solving abilities as well as prepare them for new and possibly frightening circumstances that may await them out in the 'cold, cruel world.'

But, before rushing out to order a playground built in your backyard, have a clear idea of what you want the pups to accomplish, and a well-thought-out procedure you can use to help them become quickly confident and successful in each enrichment task.

'Obstacles should be geared to your pup's age, size and breed.'

Guidelines

1. Set up very simple tasks at first, then make sure each puppy is always successful at its beginning attempts. Never

go to a more difficult or complex level until the pup is comfortable and relaxed at the introductory level.

2. Always use food as a motivator as well as a reward for successful completion of a task. Lack of interest in food often indicates stress, so if the puppies show continued interest in food, assume their stress levels are minimal.

3. Try to resist the temptation to lure the puppy through a task with food. Food is best used as a reward for the successful completion of the task, but don't hesitate to use a food lure if you have a bashful or hesitant puppy.

4. Only do each enrichment exercise three times in a row with each puppy. Then wait at least five minutes before working with the pup again. And, for very young puppies, only do three sets of three repetitions of any one task over a one hour period.

5. Gradually increase the difficulty of each enrichment task. Take a period of days to work toward the task's final level of complexity. Proceed carefully and slowly to make things more challenging!

6. Before starting, allow the pups to familiarize themselves with each obstacle or new situation by giving them ample time to walk around and sniff things out. To help each puppy succeed, start at the end or 'finish line' of an enrichment task that involves the negotiation of an obstacle. Then work the pup back towards the beginning or 'start line.'

7. When working with a raised obstacle, make sure to guide the pup with both hands instead of the leash.

8. Never push, pull, drag or shove your dog over or through an obstacle. If a pup hesitates and refuses to proceed, don't continue to coax it, instead immediately pick it up and place it at an easier position, closer to the end of the obstacle.

9. If the unexpected happens, and despite your care, a pup is inadvertently injured or frightened, make sure that before working with it again, it is physically able to perform the task easily. Take time to rebuild confidence by doing very simple tasks before returning to the task that was involved in the negative experience. Then, begin that enrichment task at the lowest possible level of difficulty.

10. Never allow young children to work with a pup and obstacles unless they are closely supervised.

Selecting, Building Puppy Obstacles

With these guidelines in mind, consider choosing and building the puppy obstacles to create stimulating, fun and challenging tasks. Bear in mind that the ones you select should be geared to your pup's age, size and breed, and that puppies should always be closely supervised and helped along during enrichment sessions. The recommended ages to begin are four to eight weeks, depending on breed and maturity.

1. Start by providing surfaces of various texture for the puppies to walk on. Cloth, plastic, wood and wire can be used indoors; crunchy leaves, grass, gravel or sawdust could be used outdoors. Remember that some of these items may make noise when stepped upon. Start the pups by placing only their hind feet on the new surface, praise them, and when they walk away from the strange stuff, immediately offer a food reward.

2. Make tunnels from cardboard boxes with their ends cut out to the pup's size. Paper roll cores, large diameter plastic plumbing pipe, duct pipe, or cardboard concrete forms can all be used as tunnels. Place the pup just inside the tunnel exit facing you, and offer a food reward along with plenty of praise when she walks out. Do three in a row, backing her further into the tunnel at each repetition. A children's collapsible play tunnel can be introduced by first holding it fully folded for the puppy to step through, and then gradually expanding it. How many in a row can you do? Yes, three is the number.

3. Make barriers at an appropriate, safe height for puppies to step, jump or scramble over. When introducing, place them halfway over the barrier set at its lowest position. We have found it is best for jump barriers to be inclined to the pups can choose for themselves a comfortable place to cross.

4. Place a small piece of bait on a hard rubber ball. For the introduction, let the puppy take the food off the ball while you're holding it, then place the ball in a corner. Once the puppy gets the idea, he'll learn to trap the ball to get the treat. This task encourages paw-eye coordination.

5. Make a low, wide ramp by covering several pieces of heavy cardboard with carpeting or toweling, then tape securely together with filament type strapping tape. The ramp can be elevated on one end using two-by-fours. When introducing, place the pup at the low end, and encourage him to walk off using praise and a food reward. Narrower, steeper, cleated wooden ramps can be used for older, better coordinated puppies. They love to charge up and down and leap off into outer space.

6. Place a small piece of bait in a large paper bag or cardboard box, and encourage the pup to find it by placing him or her halfway inside. Gradually start the pup from further away.

Remember to only do three repetitions in a row, even if the pup wants to do more.

7. Teach the puppies to get their feet wet! Start by placing a puppy in an empty bathtub with a skid-proof mat. Encourage the pup to explore the tub by using food rewards to overcome any hesitancy. Add a small amount of warm water before introducing the pup. Over the next several sessions, gradually raise the water level. Slowly acclimate the pups to the point where you can turn on the water while they are in the tub.

8. Teach the pups to negotiate stairs by first having them go down the steps. Start by placing them on the last step first, then use praise and a food reward to encourage then to walk off. Reverse the procedure for going up steps. Remember that even if a puppy is at ease with the stairs at home, it may need help in an unfamiliar location.

More Challenging Puppy Obstacles

These obstacles are recommended for pups age eight to sixteen weeks, depending on breed and maturity. As puppies become older and better coordinated, more complex and challenging obstacles can be introduced. Here is a list of enriching tasks that can be used by new puppy owners as well as breeders.

1. Teach your pup to ride on a cart or wagon. A simple cart can be made by securely taping several pieces of heavy cardboard to an equipment dolly. Start the pup out by holding the dolly in a corner to prevent movement. Gradually teach the pup to stay on the dolly by offering a food reward only when it is up on the cart. Do at least six sets of three repetitions at this level before beginning to move the cart. When first moving the cart, make sure to hold the pup securely

with your free hand, or enlist a helper. Only move the cart a few inches, then reward the pup while holding it on the cart. Do this twice more, moving the cart a little further each time. If you gradually increase the cart's movement, it won't be long until the pup will happily ride unassisted - and be the envy of the neighborhood. (A similar technique can be used to teach a puppy to ride a children's merry-go-round.)

2. Teach your pup to slide down a small child's slide by first placing her at the bottom of the slide. Encourage your pup to "slide off" using plenty of praise, while supporting her with your hands. Use a food reward when she touches the ground.

3. "Teach" your pup to swim comfortably, using a children's wading pool. Start by using the methods described to introduce the puppy to the bath tub. Gradually add more warm water so that by the end of the week, the puppy is swimming freely.

4. Teach your pup to slide down the play slide into the water by first working with each obstacle independently. Before combining them, make sure each one is mastered. Then, starting with only one-half inch of warm water in the pool, place the puppy at the very bottom of the slide. Have your camera ready!

5. Puppies that have been introduced to rigid tunnels can learn to shove through a soft cloth tunnel. You can make one by stitching 60 inch (or more) wide fabric into a tube, and inserting flexible poly pipe into a channel sewn into one end. Start by holding the tunnel with the fabric gathered up. Have a helper hold the pup, while you encourage it to step through and immediately reward this super effort with praise and a treat. Slowly extend the cloth, holding it up so they can peek through to begin with.

If you are an apartment dweller or don't have easy access to the great outdoors, challenging, fun and stimulating obstacles can be concocted from common household items.

1. Teach your pup to jump over an inclined broom stick which has been placed across a hallway. Once that challenge is conquered, progress to vacuum cleaner and turn it on.

2. Make a puppy slide by taping together thick cardboard cut from an appliance box. Join the pieces with double-faced carpet tape to ensure a smooth slide surface. Place the cardboard over a stairway and secure the top and bottom to the stairs with the double-sided tape.

3. Teach your pup to ride a puppy wagon, and then introduce him to the elevator in your building. Give him a puppy wagon ride to the elevator.

4. Folding chairs or a folding kitchen stool can be used like a ladder. Teach the pup to walk through them while they are laid flat on the floor.

5. A tunnel can be simply made from an old sheet draped over chairs or a coffee table.

There are many other obstacles and enriching, challenging tasks you can use to turn your puppies on to learning and life. The more you work with your pup using safe and effective methods, the closer that special bond will become between you. Your pup will not only be confident in facing new and challenging situations, but will learn to trust and work with you just for the fun of it. No matter what activities or goals you have planned for its future, you and your dog will be better off because you took time to enrich its early life.

About the Authors

Peter Vollmer holds a degree in psychology, concentrating on animal learning and behavior, as well as a teaching certification from Lawrence University. Starting in 1975 he has worked as a canine and feline behavior consultant through numerous veterinary clinics, and helped develop pet owner education programs for the Milwaukee Veterinary Medical Association and the Wisconsin Humane Society. He has trained and handled multiple agility champion Shelties including his dog Cole who won the 2005 NADAC National Agility Championship held in St. Louis.

Nancy Vollmer has competed in Conformation, Obedience and Agility with her Shelties and has taught puppy training classes for over 25 years. She now competes in Herding and is working toward an AKC Herding Champion title with her dog Flint. She designed and wrote the Herding Instinct certification for the American Shetland Sheepdog Association, and she was a member of AKC's Herding Development Committee, helping to write the AKC's initial herding test and trial programs in 1988.

They are currently retired and living in Escondido, CA with their dogs Trace and Flint.

Their website is https://www.superpuppy.com/index.html .

OWNER'S SECTION

Chapter 5

Preliminaries

You just brought your puppy home. Congratulations! You want him to grow up to be a stable, well-adjusted, behaviorally fit adult. If he has positive experiences, you increase his chances to become one. If you spend a few minutes several times a day, that will save you weeks and even months of time and heartbreak later on because prevention now is easier than rehabilitation later. He needs to get used to all the people, places, and things that he will encounter as an adult – and now's the time to begin that journey together.

He has left the only home he has ever known, and this transition from the breeder's home to your home is a big step for your puppy, especially sleeping at night. The first few nights may be very stressful since your puppy has left not only his home but also his mom and littermates. When he slept, he slept right next to – and sometimes on top of – his brothers and sisters where he felt secure because of their proximity and warmth. Now he is in a different place, everything is new, and he does not have his littermates to keep him company.

To make the transition easier, at night, have your puppy sleep in a crate that is right next to you – it can even be on your bed, size permitting. If the crate is too big, then put it on the floor next to your bed. Don't isolate him by putting him in the kitchen or laundry room, even if that is ultimately where he is going to sleep. He needs to feel that he's not abandoned. The crate should be his personal sanctuary since he will likely be crated when you are not home and when you cannot watch him to keep him out of mischief such as chewing your antique rug. Make him comfortable in the crate. If it's cold, then cover the crate with a blanket. If he's still cold – especially for short-haired breeds – then get him a sweater or cover him with a blanket, too.

Get him a Snuggle Puppy which has a disc that you put in the microwave and a battery-powered heartbeat. If you do not have a Snuggle Puppy, then the old standby of a hot water bottle covered with a towel and a ticking clock should help. Hopefully, you have gotten some towels from your breeder that she has rubbed on her body as well as his mom and littermates, and you can put the towel in the crate, too. Roll it up and put rubber bands on the ends so it cannot unroll. (You can also use a stuffed sock.) Then put the towel into a corner of the crate to act as a bolster.

Another reason to keep the crate next to you at night is because his muscles have not developed yet, so he cannot "hold it" all night. Since dogs don't like to pee and poop in their beds – unless they're forced to because when ya gotta go, ya gotta go – you will want the crate next to you at night so when he wakes up to tell you he's gotta go, you can take him to his potty area immediately.

Why do I need to socialize and habituate him now?

Hopefully, your breeder or rescue has already begun to socialize and habituate your puppy. (Go to the Breeder section to see the exercises I recommend for breeders as well as reading the Vollmers' article on environmental enrichment.) If not, you have a lot of work to do in a very short time, especially if your puppy came from a country or rural setting and you live in the city (and vice versa) because the sights, sounds, and smells are very different. The familiarization/sensitive window closes at 16 weeks. If you accustom him to a multitude of situations before that time, then you "immunize" him for novel situations – he has many experiences to draw from so that when he encounters anything new, he will feel comfortable rather than frightened.

Adult dogs see things as either safe or dangerous – what he's been exposed to in a positive way while he's a puppy he thinks is safe, and everything else is dangerous. What's happening is that while he is a puppy, his brain cells are making connections – the more good connections, i.e., the foundation, that are made, the more behaviorally fit and stable he will be as an adult. It's the difference between building your house on chicken wire or building it on concrete. Which would you rather have as a foundation?

But sometimes, life interferes with good intentions. Your puppy gets sick or breaks a leg, which makes it difficult to give him the "outside" experiences he needs. Or maybe you become incapacitated. The problem is that he's only going to be a puppy once, and the lessons he learns now will carry through for the rest of his life – and you cannot "make up for it" later. As you continue reading, you will find many exercises that are easy and fun for both you and your puppy even if you cannot take him outside. But this book also shows you how to take him outdoors so it is safe for him.

Your job is to introduce him to as many new things as you can now. What follows are some tips, do's and don'ts, what counts and what doesn't count as socialization, an Owner Checklist – and a whole lot more.

If you're a dieter or watch your food intake, you've probably heard the phrase, "A moment on the lips, a lifetime on the hips," which means even though that chocolate cake tastes delicious right at this moment, you won't see the extra pounds right away. Socialization and habituation are like that (but in a good way) because you may not see the effects right away, but they sure will show up later on. Socialization and habituation have more impact now because this is the period in his life when he learns the most. He's only going to be a puppy once, and the lessons he learns here will carry through for the rest of his life and be a pleasure to be around.

One Hour in Our Lives

Before we get to that, I want to illustrate one day – actually one hour in my and my dogs' lives. I walk them three or four times a day for about one hour total time. During that time, every day they encounter new experiences.

Just for fun, I decided to inventory only the things that I noticed that were **different from the day before**, things I saw and heard and to some extent smelled. Our dogs' perception of the world is different from ours because their primary sense is smell while ours is sight. I have included here things that I saw and to a lesser extent smelled.

I have included ages and races of people because each encounter is different for our dogs. Dogs can tell how old someone is both by looking at their size and by their scent. Dogs may also be able to identify people by their race because different races eat different core foods, which smell differently to dogs (although many of us including myself eat anything that tastes good and have a multi-cultural palate!).

- Someone going through the garbage looking for plastic bottles
- Homeless man
- Man on a bicycle exercising his Akita
- Pile of leaves
- Bike tied to lamp post
- Bird poop
- Crows flying and pecking at grass
- Middle aged man walking small black dog
- The smell of coffee brewing
- Older woman walking two Yorkies
- Young Caucasian woman walking black and white aggressive mid-sized dog
- Hispanic man walking French bulldog
- Asian woman walking Shiba Inu
- Teenage male with baseball cap on skateboard
- Candy bar wrapper
- Motorcycle
- Garbage truck
- Hispanic woman walking little boy to school
- African-American female school crossing guard
- For Rent sign
- Styrofoam plate on the ground
- Fast food cup with straw
- Young Caucasian man getting into car
- Asian man opening trunk of car
- Newly-planted flowers
- Garbage cans set at the curb for pickup
- Sprinklers watering grass

- Metal security door closing
- Teenage girl talking on phone
- Cigarette butts on the ground
- Middle-aged woman smoking
- Blind Asian woman with service dog
- Large branch broken and hanging from the tree
- Shopping cart on the sidewalk
- Old sofa by the curb
- Dogs barking from a balcony
- Three elderly men jogging down the street
- Car racing down the street
- Old baby seat left outside
- The smell of baking bread
- Tow truck
- Man pushing vacuum cleaner
- Crumpled up paper on the ground (People seem to be slobs in my neighborhood.......)
- Motorcycle
- Teenage girl washing car on the lawn (honest!)
- Old newspapers
- Candy wrappers
- Dog barking from inside a house
- African-American female postal worker pushing cart
- Two men working on car engine
- The smell of grilling chicken
- Apartment for rent sign
- Trees being trimmed
- Wood chipper
- Car backfiring

- Horns honking
- Palm fronds on ground

Again, these were different experiences from the previous day, included pretty much in the order that they happened as we were walking. My dogs took them in stride because they are exposed to novel events every day. There are many, many things that I have omitted, the first one coming to mind is the different cars and trucks that passed us were definitely not the same nor were they in the same order as yesterday – and, of course, the smells. But you get the picture.

Chapter 6

"I Don't Need to Socialize My Puppy"

Trainers, including myself, sometimes have a difficult time letting their clients know about the importance of puppy socialization and habituation. Frequently, there is some excuse as to why they can't, won't, or don't want to take their puppies out to experience the real world. I am very grateful to **Dr. Ian Dunbar** who generously gave me permission to use his article from www.DogStarDaily.com which addresses the most common excuses, which follow.

"Our last dog was perfectly trustworthy."

Maybe you were just lucky and picked a born-to-be-perfect puppy. Or maybe you were an excellent trainer. But can you still remember what you did back then and do you still have the time to do it?

"Our last dog just loved kids!"

One young family doted on their first dog and devoted a lot of time to his training. The whole family attended puppy classes and held puppy parties at home for the children's friends. So many children spent time playing games and reward-training the dog, that of course the dog loved children. The dog enjoyed his sunset years proudly watching the children grow up and graduate from high school. By the time the parents got their second dog, the children had all left the nest. The new puppy grew up in a world without children. All went well for many years — that is, until grandchildren appeared on the scene.

"He's fine with me."

Wonderful! Certainly the first step of socialization is to make sure the puppy is perfectly friendly with the family. But it is imperative that the pup become Mr. Sociable with friends, neighbors, visitors, and strangers so that he does not object to being examined by the veterinarian or playfully grabbed and hugged by children.

"Our pup gets more than enough socialization with our family."

Not true! In order to be accepting of strangers as an adult, your puppy needs to meet at least three unfamiliar people each day, not the same people over and over again.

"I don't have any friends to help me socialize my puppy."

Well, you soon will. Socializing your puppy will do wonders for your social life. Invite your neighbors over to meet the pup. Invite people over from work. Check out the puppy classes in your area and invite over some puppy owners from there. They will more than appreciate the problems you are about to encounter in the future. If you cannot get people to come to your home to meet the puppy, take him to safe places to meet people. Do not put him on the ground in public places that may have been frequented by unvaccinated adult dogs until he is at least three months old and current with his vaccinations. Buy a soft carrier and take your puppy on errands: for example, to the bank, the bookstore, or hardware store. See if you can take your puppy to work. Later on, you will be able to take your pup to puppy classes, to dog parks, and on neighborhood walks. But he needs to meet lots of people right away. So whatever you do, do not keep your puppy a secret.

"I don't want my dogs to accept food treats from strangers."

Perhaps your concern is that someone may poison the dog. As a rule, dogs are only poisoned when left alone in backyards — because they are not housetrained and therefore cannot be left safely indoors — or when let loose to range and roam. But you are not inviting dog-hating strangers to interact with your puppy. Instead, you are inviting over selected family, neighbors, and friends. Regardless, every puppy should be taught never to touch or take any object, including food, from any person's hand unless first the puppy hears "Rover, Take it," or some such command. Having learned these basic manners, your dog will only accept food from people who know his name and who know the appropriate take it command — namely, from family and friends.

"I don't want my dog to like strangers. I want him to protect me."

Oh, come on ... try telling that to your veterinarian, or to your children's friends' parents. However, if you mean you want your dog to perform some protective function, that's a different matter. But surely you are not going to leave it up to a poorly socialized dog to make decisions regarding whom to protect, whom to protect against, and how to protect. Any good protection dog has first been super-socialized to the point of total confidence, and then carefully taught how, when, and whom to protect. Training your dog to bark or growl on command is a more than sufficient protective deterrent. Your dog may be taught to vocalize in certain situations: for example, when somebody steps onto your property or touches your car. Alarm barkers are extremely effective deterrents, especially if they do not bark when people simply walk by your house or car.

[This is my P.S. to Dr. Dunbar's comments – a dog who has not been familiarized to different types and ages of people will likely protect himself before he will protect you! He will run away from a threat.]

"I don't have the time."

Then give the puppy to someone who does have the time! This puppy may still be saved if someone is willing to take the time to socialize him.

"I need to dominate my pup to get him to respect me."

Not necessarily. Or, not at all. If you physically force and dominate your puppy, he won't respect you. He may heed your commands — grudgingly and fearfully — but he certainly won't respect you. More likely, your dog will grow to resent you.

Besides, there are easy and enjoyable ways to get your dog to show respect. Years ago in one of my puppy classes, I remember a young couple who had a four-year-old daughter named Kristen and a Rottweiler named Panzer. In class, Kristen had the dog better trained than her parents and could consistently get Panzer to come, sit, lie down, and roll over. Kristen would give Panzer a tummy rub when he was lying on his side and he would raise his hind leg to expose his belly. Kristen would talk to Panzer in a squeaky little voice. Kristin squeaked, and Panzer did what she asked. Or, we could say that Kristen requested and Panzer agreed. Or, that Kristen commanded and Panzer obeyed. More important, though, Panzer happily and willingly complied. And when it comes to children training dogs, happy willing compliance is the only kind of compliance that is safe and makes sense. Was Kristen dominating Panzer? Absolutely! But in a much more effective way than by using brute force. As a child, Kristen had to use brain instead of brawn to control Panzer's behavior. Kristen mentally dominated Panzer's will.

Kristen's training engendered Panzer's respect and friendship. Panzer respected her wishes. Also, by approaching promptly off-leash, Panzer demonstrated that he liked Kristen. By sitting and lying down, Panzer showed that he really liked Kristen and wanted to stay close to her. By rolling over, Panzer displayed appeasement. And by lifting his leg to expose his inguinal area, Panzer displayed deference. In doggy language, exposing the inguinal region means, "I am a lowly worm. I respect your higher rank, and I would like to be friends." If you want your puppy to respect you, lure/reward train him to come, sit, lie down, and roll over. If you want your puppy to show deference, teach him to lick your hand or shake hands. Licking and pawing are both active appeasement gestures — signs of wanting to be friends. If you would like your puppy to show doggy deference, tickle his goolies when he is lying on his side and watch him raise his hind leg to expose his inguinal area.

"Dogs of this breed are particularly hard to handle."

Using this excuse to give up on handling, gentling, and socialization exercises is too silly for words. If your research on dog breeds has convinced you that you truly have a difficult breed, you should double or triple the socialization and handling exercises, wind back all developmental deadlines, and start each batch of exercises earlier. Strangely enough, though, I have heard this excuse given for just about every breed of dog. As soon as you think that your chosen breed is too much dog for you, seek help immediately. Find a trainer who can teach you how to handle your puppy before you cause irreparable damage to his temperament.

"My spouse/significant other/parent/child selected the most dominant pup in the litter."

Did you remember the cardinal rule of puppy selection, that all family members completely agree? Well, it's a bit late for that now, and so I would suggest the same advice as above. As soon as you suspect you have a difficult pup, double or triple the socialization and handling exercises and start each batch of exercises earlier. Additionally, you might consider learning how to train your spouse, significant other, parent, or child.

"Something is genetically wrong with the puppy."

Same advice as above: as soon as you suspect your puppy has some kind of organic problem, double or triple the socialization and handling exercises and start each batch of exercises earlier. It's a bit late for genetic screening, and, in any case, what else can you do —tweak the dog's genes? Many people use breed, dominance, or organic conditions as an excuse to give up on the pup — and as an excuse to not socialize and train him. In reality, socialization and training is the puppy's only hope. Your puppy needs socialization and training. Lots of it! Right away! Regardless of breed and breeding, and regardless of your puppy's socialization and training prior to coming to your home, as of right now, any change in your puppy's temperament, behavior, or manners is completely dependent on how you socialize and train him. Work with your puppy and he will get better. Don't work with your puppy and he will get worse. Your puppy's future is entirely in your hands.

"He's just a puppy!" or, "He's sooooo cute!" or, "He's only playing!" or, "He'll grow out of it!"

Of course your puppy is only playing — play-barking, play-growling, play-biting, play-fighting, play-protecting a bone, or playing tug-of-war. If you just laugh at him, your pup will continue playing the aggression game as he grows older, and in no time at all, your fully grown adult dog will be playing for real. Puppy play is all important. Play is essential if a puppy is to learn the social relevance of the vast jumble of behaviors in his doggy repertoire, specifically the appropriateness and inappropriateness of each behavior in each setting. In a sense, play enables a pup to learn what he can get away with. What you need to do is teach your puppy the rules of the game. And the more rules he learns in puppyhood, the safer he will be as an adult dog. Puppy barking and growling are quite normal and acceptable, just as long as you can stop the noise when you wish. Stopping an eight-week-old puppy from barking or growling is pretty easy. Be still yourself, so the puppy may calm down more easily. Say, "Puppy, Shush!" and waggle a food treat in front of his nose. Say, "Good dog," and offer the treat when the pup eventually shushes. Similarly, tug-of-war is a normal and acceptable game, just as long as your pup never initiates the game and you can get the pup to release the object and sit at any time. Both are easy rules to teach to an eight-week-old puppy. When playing tug-of-war, instruct your puppy to release the object and sit at least every minute. Periodically stop tugging, say, "Thank you," and waggle a food treat in front of his nose. When the puppy releases the object to sniff the treat, praise him, and ask him to sit. When he sits, praise him profusely, offer the food treat, and then resume the game.

Euphemism, Litotes, and Other Outrageous Silliness! "He takes a while to warm to strangers!" "He's not overly fond of children!" and "He's a bit hand-shy!"

How can anyone live with a dog knowing that he is stressed by the presence of strangers and children and scared of human hands? The poor dog must be in a state of extreme anxiety. Just how many times does this dog have to beg, implore, and warn you that he feels uncomfortable around strangers and children and does not like people reaching for his collar? This is simply an accident waiting to happen. What if an unfamiliar child should reach for the dog's collar, possibly around the dog's food bowl, when the dog is having a bad-hair day and not feeling good? A dog bite for sure. What will we say? That the dog bit without warning and without reason? The poor dog had at least five good reasons to bite: (1) a stranger, (2) a child, (3) reaching for his collar, (4) proximity to his food bowl, and (5) not feeling good. And the dog had been warning his family repeatedly for some time. If there is anything that upsets your puppy, desensitize him to that specific stimulus or scenario immediately. Help your puppy build his confidence so that he may approach everyday events without stress or fear. The required confidence-building exercises have all been described. Use them!

About the Author

Veterinarian, animal behaviorist, and dog trainer, **Ian Dunbar, Ph.D., BSc, BVetMed, MRCVS** received his veterinary degree and a Special Honors degree in Physiology & Biochemistry from the Royal Veterinary College (London University) plus a doctorate in animal behavior from the Psychology Department at UC Berkeley, where he researched the development of social hierarchies and aggression in domestic dogs.

In 1982, Dr. Dunbar designed and taught the world's very first off-leash puppy socialization and training classes, SIRIUS Puppy Training. Subsequently, he developed the San Francisco SPCA's Animal Behavior Department, started the American Kennel Club's Gazette "Behavior" column, and founded the Association of Pet Dog Trainers. He has authored numerous books and DVDs about puppy/dog behavior and training. Currently, Dr. Dunbar is the Scientific Director for http://www.DogStarDaily.com, a free online, multi-media educational website for puppy and dog owners, as well as giving seminars around the world.

****

In addition to Dr. Dunbar's excellent responses to typical excuses, I have a couple to add.

"I live in the country and my dog is not going to meet a lot of people."

Yes, he will. What about your vet, your friends, mail carriers, delivery people, repair people? You may live in the country, but you aren't a hermit!

"I live in the city so he will get socialized by going everywhere I do."

You're right up to a point – it's good that he will be introduced to several new experiences, but just because they're new experiences does not mean that they're good experiences. It's your job to set up those new experiences so they are positive experiences.

"My puppy loves everyone."

You are lucky that he loves people – but does he love people because they are introduced to him inside your house? What happens when he is taken outside to a place that he is not familiar with and that person wears some clothing that he has never seen? It's like a cocoon inside your house where everything is pretty much under your control. And then he goes outside where much less is under your control – there's buses that race by and people carrying umbrellas and little kids screaming. There's so much more stimulation outside. What happens if a motorcycle goes by when he is meeting your elderly neighbor who walks with a cane for the first time? That motorcycle noise is scary, so now whenever he meets an elderly person or a person walking with a cane, he's going to be scared.

"My vet says I shouldn't take him outside until he's had all his shots"

This one is so important I've devoted the next chapter to it.

"Now that he's 16 weeks old, I can stop socializing him."

Nope. Introducing your puppy to a human world is an ongoing process; it cannot be done in an afternoon, a week, or even 16 weeks. What counts is if your dog has new experiences daily, which means new people, new places, new dogs. It's daily for the rest of his life. That's why taking him for a walk daily is so important. Yes, the time when he is most receptive is before 16 weeks, but if he is not introduced to new things after that, then his comfort level drops. It really is "use it or lose it"!

Chapter 7

"But My Vet Says I Shouldn't Take My Puppy Outside Until He's Had All His Shots"

Your veterinarian is likely your first animal care professional you visit after the breeder or rescue, and it is essential for your puppy to be examined medically and then vaccinated. While you are at your vet's office, it is logical to ask him or her about behavior issues with puppies – and there are a lot of them! (Please refer to Normal and Abnormal Behavior in Appendix 4.)

I have the utmost respect and admiration for veterinarians. They try to be helpful by giving advice similar to what worked for their personal dogs or by giving advice on what they think may work. Most vets when they are in vet school study medicine, not behavior. There are only 46 Certified Veterinary Behaviorists in the US as compared to 102,744 veterinarians. It seems logical that some vets refer to other dog professionals because they realize it's out of their field of expertise. (Yay, I like these vets!)

At the same time, many veterinarians recommend not taking your puppy into the real world until he's had all his shots – and those shots are not finished until he is four months old, which is past the important social and environmental exposure periods we have been talking about. Your vet is interested in your dog from a medical standpoint, and I am interested in him from a behavioral standpoint. It is crucial to take him outdoors before he has had all his shots so he can become acclimated to the sights, sounds, places, situations, and smells in his neighborhood. As has been demonstrated first by Scott and Fuller and reiterated by many other behaviorists and clinicians, waiting until your puppy has completed his vaccines to take him outdoors makes it difficult for him to accept new situations in his environment. Because of this, many vets are changing their opinions and have begun to work in conjunction with trainers to offer classes for puppies.

The **American Veterinary Society of Animal Behavior** in 2003 recognized that more puppies are euthanized for behavior issues than medical ones and officially changed its position, saying that, "The primary and most important time for puppy socialization is the first three months of life…. It should be the standard of care for puppies to receive such socialization before they are fully vaccinated." The entire AVSAB position statement appears here. http://tinyurl.com/q3u6mpz

So the times, they are a changin', and veterinary schools and especially veterinary conferences are beginning to reflect the change. I looked at the curriculum for several veterinary colleges, and there were only one or two classes in their curriculum dealing with behavior out of dozens and dozens of classes dealing not only with veterinary science but also everything from veterinary legal issues to sea turtles. I was delighted to discover that at the Wild West Veterinary Conference in October 2013, there were 15 seminars relating to behavior out of 82 total seminars. The 2014 Tufts Veterinary Conference on the Genetic Basis for Canine Behavior was held in conjunction with the International Association of Animal Behavior Consultants – yippee! This is a huge leap forward.

True story – I was speaking with a veterinary student, and she said something that had never crossed my mind. Vet school is four years. It's always been four years. It's much more difficult to become a veterinarian than to become a human doctor because in four years, students have to learn about anatomy, physiology, surgical procedures, nutrition, and much more for many different species of animals including farm animals, wildlife, and companion animals. Phew! The amount that vet students (and veterinarians) have to learn is exponentially greater than just a few years ago, not only in school but also in keeping up with medical advancements in journals and conferences. Is it any wonder that most veterinarians keep up with current knowledge in their chosen field – veterinary medicine – rather than behavior?

Dr. R.K. Anderson, DVM, Diplomat, American College of Veterinary Preventive Medicine and Diplomat of American College of Veterinary Behaviorists was the first veterinary behaviorist to advocate that puppies should become acclimated to the outside world after owners take them home. Dr. Anderson was instrumental in advocating puppy classes, and he wrote a letter to other veterinarians, which appears below:

TO: My Colleagues in Veterinary Medicine:

Common questions I receive from puppy owners, dog trainers and veterinarians concern: 1) what is the most favorable age or period of time when puppies learn best? 2) what are the health implications of my advice that veterinarians and trainers should offer socialization programs for puppies starting at 8 to 9 weeks of age.

Puppies begin learning at birth and their brains appear to be particularly responsive to learning and retaining experiences that are encountered during the first 13 to 16 weeks after birth. This means that breeders, new puppy owners, veterinarians, trainers and behaviorists have a responsibility to assist in providing these learning/socialization experiences with other puppies/dogs, with children/adults and with various environmental situations during this optimal period from birth to 16 weeks.

Many veterinarians are making this early socialization and learning program part of a total wellness plan for breeders and new owners of puppies during the first 16 weeks of a puppy's life -- the first 7-8 weeks with the breeder and the next 8 weeks with the new owners. This socialization program should enroll puppies from 8 to 12 weeks of age as a key part of any preventive medicine program to improve the bond between pets and their people and keep dogs as valued members of the family for 12 to 18 years.

To take full advantage of this early special learning period, many veterinarians recommend that new owners take their puppies to puppy socialization classes, beginning at 8 to 9 weeks of age. At this age they should have (and can be required to have) received a minimum of their first series of vaccines for protection against infectious diseases. This provides the basis for increasing immunity by further repeated exposure to these antigens either through natural exposure in small doses or artificial exposure with vaccines during the next 8 to 12 weeks. In addition the owner and people offering puppy socialization should take precautions to have the environment and the participating puppies as free of natural exposure as possible by good hygiene and caring by careful instructors and owners.

Experience and epidemiologic data support the relative safety and lack of transmission of disease in these puppy socialization classes over the past 10 years in many parts of the United States. In fact; the risk of a dog dying because of infection with distemper or parvo disease is far less than the much higher risk of a dog dying (euthanasia) because of a behavior problem. Many veterinarians are now offering new puppy owners puppy socialization classes in their hospitals or nearby training facilities in conjunction with trainers and behaviorists because they want socialization and training to be very important parts of a wellness plan for every puppy. We need to recognize that this special sensitive period for learning is the best opportunity we have to influence behavior for dogs and the most important and longest lasting part of a total wellness plan.

Are there risks? Yes. But 10 years of good experience and data, with few exceptions, offers veterinarians the opportunity to generally recommend early socialization and training classes, beginning when puppies are 8 to 9 weeks of age. However, we always follow a veterinarian's professional judgment, in individual cases or situations, where special circumstances warrant further immunization for a special puppy before starting such classes. During any period of delay for puppy classes, owners should begin a program of socialization with children and adults, outside their family, to take advantage of this special period in a puppy's life.

If there are further questions, veterinarians may call me at 651-644-7400 for discussion and clarification. [Sadly, Dr. Anderson died in 2012.]

Robert K. Anderson DVM

Diplomate ACVB and ACVPM

Professor and Director Emeritus, Animal Behavior Clinic and

Center to Study Human/Animal Relationships and Environments

University of Minnesota

If your veterinarian advocates isolation of your puppy until he has completed his puppy vaccines, please show them Dr. Anderson's letter and AVSAB's position.

Your Puppy's First Veterinary Visit

Keeping all that in mind, your puppy's very first vet visit should be a social visit and a wellness checkup, not one where he gets vaccinated. Make an appointment when it is not busy so the vet and staff can pay a bit more attention to your puppy. Carry him into the office – don't let him walk on the ground in the parking lot, on the grass, or in the waiting room because sick dogs come into the office, and you do not want him to pick up germs on his feet. When you are waiting, keep him in your arms or in a crate, but not on the floor. You want him to be comfortable going to the vet's, so ask the staff to examine him on the table, weigh him, give him an exam where they look in his ears, eyes, teeth, and pinch his body where he is likely to get vaccinated. All this time you are giving him treats. Plus the office staff will likely fuss over him, too, so now your puppy's first vet visit has been an enjoyable one.

Chapter 8

The Fundamental Plan
along with Do's and Don'ts

The Fundamental Plan is environmental enrichment inside your house and habituation outside your house. Simply, **Environmental Enrichment** provides your puppy with a multitude of experiences to see and do and interact with inside your house. **Habituation** helps him become comfortable about novel experiences both inside and outside your house.

Environmental Enrichment can generally be divided into five areas:

- Food-based Enrichment
- Sensory Enrichment
- Social Enrichment
- Novel Items
- Positive Training

We're going to concentrate on the first four because there are a gazillion books on training and other puppy issues. Hopefully, the place where you got your puppy did the exercises in the Breeder section of this book. I would encourage you to read that section both to get more ideas and to fill in the blanks where you think your puppy might need them. (I can't think of everything!)

BUT you still need to continue to introduce him to new things for several reasons:

- His brain is still growing fast, and he's making the connections between the neurons in his brain. (Puppies with more neural connections have larger brains as adults.)
- You are building a relationship and bonding with your puppy.
- You've heard the saying, "Use it or lose it," and it could never be more applicable than it is here.
- He is in a completely new environment with new sights, sounds, smells, and people. For most of your dog's life, when he learns something new, it is very specific to the place that he learned it because he takes a "mental picture" of what he is looking at (the people present, the smells, the sounds, the location) and that picture does not transfer well without many repetitions.

(As an aside, that principle also holds true for training. In other words, if he learned Sit in the living room when you were standing up, he needs to be taught Sit again in the kitchen. If he learned Sit in the living room when you were standing up, he needs to be retaught Sit when you are sitting down because *you* have changed your position from standing to sitting. If he learned Sit in the living room when you were alone, he does not know Sit if there is another dog or another person present. It takes at least 50 reps before he understands what Sit means wherever he is.)

While your dog is a puppy, these associations generalize to other places much more readily than if he learns later. For example, if he learned that dropping pots and pans in the breeder's kitchen was no big deal, then hearing a similar sound in your house or dealing with motorcycles or cars that backfire outside will not be as traumatic since he has acclimated to loud sounds.

Your job now is to familiarize your puppy with his new human world and help him be comfortable with anything new before he is 16 weeks old so he:

- Learns to recognize and interact with the people and other animals he is living with

- Develops the communication skills to recognize whether he is being threatened

- Recognizes and responds to the intentions of others

- Becomes accustomed to his environment

- Learns to ignore nonthreatening things in the environment

What are your puppy's personality and temperament?

Just because your puppy comes from one of the breeds that is "friendly and good with everyone" does not mean that he is going to be that way without being socialized and habituated. (If your puppy's mom was friendly – or fearful – then there's a high probability that your puppy will have the same temperament because he has inherited her genes and spent a lot of time with her before he came into your home. That's why it's important to meet the mom before getting a puppy.)

With new experiences, depending on his personality, your puppy will:

- Ignore it totally

- Run up to it to check it out

  Look at it and slowly approach

- Bark at it
- Run away

All of the responses that I just described can come from different puppies from the same litter. Whatever genes he has simply primes the pump, so to speak. What your breeder/rescue has done and what you do now will fuel the car.

Every dog, just like every person, is an individual and has his own personality and temperament. (I'll bet you know siblings where you scratch your head and wonder how they could ever be related since they are so different.) There is a range of possible personalities:

- Your puppy loves everyone and/or is not afraid of anything. He acts first and thinks later – if he thinks at all. (With this puppy, your role is to "curb his enthusiasm" and get him to focus on you.) I recommend a solid obedience foundation as well as the Space exercises in My Smart Puppy by **Brian Kilcommons** and **Sarah Wilson**.

- Your puppy seems just to like your family and nobody else and/or he is generally okay in new surroundings. (With this category and the next two categories, you can help him along by pairing up good stuff with the things he is wary around – more on that later.)

- Your puppy just likes you and/or he is not comfortable around new people or things. (Your work is **really** cut out for you because he needs as many new positive experiences as he can get.)

- Your puppy does not like a certain category of people. Here are just a few examples.
    o Women but not men – or vice versa
    o A certain race or ethnicity
    o Adults but not children
    o People carrying things or walking funny
    o People in uniforms
    o People who gesture a lot
    o People who are loud

- Your puppy is aloof and ignores everybody and just does his own thing all the time. (With this puppy, the first place I would go is to the vet to see that he is medically okay. For example, if he's deaf, he cannot hear you, so it's not a question of ignoring.) If he is okay, then you are going to have a *very* difficult time helping him bond with you and ultimately training him. My suggestion, sad as it may be, is that this is not a good fit and he should be returned to where you got him.

The Do's

- Give him a few days to orient to your household and the rhythms of your life and then start the exercises. The perfect outcome is that he forms a positive association with each new encounter, but it's okay if it's neutral.
- Have him checked out by your veterinarian to ensure that any medical issues do not interfere with his learning.
- Take it easy. Don't do too much at once. The first few times he goes outside may be difficult because he can be overwhelmed by everything being new. Taking the time for him to be comfortable around one new experience is better than rushing him through several.

- Let him explore at his own pace. Don't force your puppy into doing anything.

- Plan carefully – and you do need a plan; it should not be haphazard. Nothing should be harmful and frightening. Socializing your puppy is not a social time for you. It's a time to pay attention to your puppy. If he is frightened, then you should notice that immediately and not be ensconced in a conversation with your friend. Be prepared to leave the area if you think the situation is overwhelming for your puppy.

- Your agenda should be to have him encounter at least ten new things every day, both inside and outside your house. Some of these will be everyday occurrences – your hair dryer, a vacuum cleaner, opening and closing doors and drawers, hearing traffic, seeing squirrels, and passing people on the street. But some may not – dropping pots and pans, interacting with children, seeing a moving van.

- You can overwhelm your puppy by doing too much at one time or too much every day. Take him out for five to ten minutes several times a day rather than an hour at a time because that is just too much stimulation for him to absorb. You may, however, increase the length of the time as he gets older.

- Do easy things first, make sure your puppy is comfortable, and then build on those experiences by making them more complicated.

- Act the way you want your puppy to act. If you want him to be confident and happy, then you act confident and happy.

- Be sure to match the situation you are introducing him to something he can handle. For example, if he's frightened of loud noises in your house and you've never taken him outside, then don't go where a motorcycle is roaring down the street.

- If he seems hesitant or unsure, let him go up to whatever he is concerned with at his own pace and retreat if he wants. Your job is to reward positive experiences with praise, petting, and treats as he gets close. If he will not eat treats, then he is likely too stressed.

- What may be okay for a confident puppy may be overwhelming for a shy puppy. His experiences should be fun and rewarding for him.

- Remember that he does go through Fear Periods. If you think he is fearful of something that he readily accepted yesterday, he may be experiencing a Fear Period.

- Try to make sure he's empty, i.e., he's pottied, when taking him to new places.

- Try to use food as a reward rather than a lure.

- Use common sense where you take him, but don't be over protective.

- It's possible that he can react strongly to new experiences outdoors, and you may be surprised and even embarrassed by his behavior. Rather than be embarrassed, why not chalk this up as a learning experience for both of you? If he's extremely fearful, then you may be going too fast. Read appendices 6 and 7 on Fear and Targeting, or you may need to contact a behavior consultant who is familiar with working with fear behaviors.

- One last point, and this is about indoors. He also should learn how to be comfortable and occupy himself when he is alone. I like to use exercise pens for this. He will sleep most of the time, but when he wakes up, after he eliminates, he wants to be occupied. He needs to learn that you are not going to pay attention to him 100% of the time. When you determine what his favorite toys and puzzles are, let him have them only when he is inside the Xpen so he is not left with nothing to do. The pen should not be a jail, and he does need supervised time outside where he can run around and exercise.

The Don'ts

- Don't take your puppy in the woods or on vacant lots. (There is an exception – if you plan to hunt or camp with your dog, then he should be familiar with the outdoor areas he will be in, and your breeder should have begun the process and instructed you on what to do. However, just to be on the safe side, I would wait at least a week after he has had his second set of vaccines to give his body a chance to build up immunity before taking him into the woods. And be sure to check whether there have been any cases of rabies reported in the area because the rabies vaccine is the last shot after the puppy shots. Don't go anywhere that has a history of rabies or other diseases such as distemper or parvo.)

- Don't take your puppy where unknown dogs have walked. (He can pick up diseases on his feet and then lick his feet and become infected.)

- Don't let him walk into your vet's office or on the lawn, sidewalk, or parking lot around the office. Carry him or keep him in a crate.

- Don't punish him if he barks at something. That's simply information telling you to work on acclimating to that. Keep him on the periphery and then go closer as he gets comfortable. (See Fear and Targeting in appendices 6 and 7 for more information.)

- Unless there is some immediate danger to him or to you, don't drag him towards or away from anything.

- Puppies love to sniff things on the ground, but this is not the time for that, especially if it is poop.

- Don't protect him from something he thinks is scary or regard fear as a setback. Again, it is information to see where you need to help him. If you do not help him and give him the opportunity to overcome it now, he will never have the confidence to overcome it when he is older and is more likely to become a fear aggressive dog.

If, despite all your efforts your puppy, is fearful or aggressive, find a trainer or behavior consultant immediately. This is too important to wait.

Remember that you're doing these exercises before your dog is fully immunized, so his body has not built up the antibodies necessary to fight diseases and he needs to be protected. One other thing – your puppy is vulnerable for the first 48 hours at a minimum after he is vaccinated while his body is producing those antibodies, the process taking about two weeks. So be *especially* careful for the first few days after being vaccinated.

> **True story** – One of my clients had two tiny puppies, and she waited until they had their last shots to take them to see the real world. They got their final puppy vaccines in the morning, and she took them on a five-mile walk that same afternoon – no kidding! Both puppies developed parvo. Although I had cautioned her beforehand to wait, unfortunately, all she remembered was that it was okay to take them out after the last vaccine. Both puppies survived, but it cost her over $7,000.

With that in mind, until two weeks after they are fully vaccinated, don't go to:

- Adoption events
- Any area of town that dogs are allowed to run loose or where there are packs of dogs
- Anyplace that you feel uncomfortable taking him
- Anyplace that other dogs have peed or pooped

- Boarding kennels
- Dog parks
- Dog shelters and rescues
- Dog shows
- Pet stores unless he is on a towel or carrier in a cart
- Public parks with dogs

For your puppy's safety, don't take him to a class:

- In a pet store, especially ones that have adoption events (I wholly support adoption events and getting puppies from rescue groups – all of my own dogs have been rescues. However, your responsibility is to your puppy and not to expose him to any medical issues that these rescues may have.)
- That does not
  o Make you wait at least two weeks after your puppy comes into your home
  o Check his immunization status
  o Check for a negative fecal test.

This is for your puppy's safety as well as the safety of the other puppies because if any of them has any parasites, worms, or diseases, those should make themselves known in two weeks.

Finally, don't let him play with a puppy or dog (especially one that is newly adopted) unless that puppy/dog has been vaccinated and has a negative fecal test.

What doesn't count?

Each experience needs to be something new so that a new connection is made between brain cells. It doesn't count:

- If you take your puppy to the same place day after day
- If you have a lot of company coming into your house (Yes, it's better that he gets used to new people *inside* your house, but he needs to get used to people *outside*, too.)
- If the same people come into your house over and over again
- If your puppy plays with the same dog again and again
- If he gets along with your kids
- If you stop taking him out even after he is 16 weeks old

Does it help if you do these things once or twice? Maybe. But he needs *new* encounters.

Exercises to Do Inside Your Home

Sometimes you cannot take your puppy outside because of the weather. Maybe you are ill or immobile; see if you can get someone to help you with these exercises. If your puppy is ill and is totally incapacitated, then obviously this is not the time to venture outside or to try to teach him something. Wait until he feels better. However, maybe he has a broken leg – his brain is okay, so you can do many of the exercises outlined here with just a little effort that will pay off big time for your puppy. Some of these suggestions you probably would be doing in the course of everyday living but not realize that you are actually helping your puppy because you are giving him new experiences.

Many of us pride ourselves in keeping a neat house where there is a place for everything and everything is in its place. Great for us, boring for our dogs. How often do you move your sofa or rearrange furniture in the bedroom? If you're like me, hardly at all. It would be great for your puppy – but impractical for you – to move your furniture around on a daily basis.

> **True story** – I had a client who called me because her dog had separation anxiety. The dog barked at me when I came into his house and then ran into the other room to hide. I put my purse on the sofa and sat down at the dining room table to talk with my client. After about 15 minutes, the dog came into the living room and saw my purse on the sofa and barked at it hysterically. The owner then said that she could not move anything out of place in the house because the dog had memorized where all the furniture was and became unglued when it wasn't exactly how he left it. I don't want your dog to become like this poor dog.

This is a time when we can be slobs – and you have my permission! Why? Because your puppy needs to see many changes both inside and outside his house. He likely is going to spend more time inside than outside, and with most of us, inside barely changes. But we can make things change!

A couple of caveats

Make sure you supervise him (That means keeping your eyeballs on him, not on the computer, TV, or your phone!) when he is interacting with these items – such as finding treats in boxes – because you don't want him chewing the boxes.

Everything that he interacts with should be clean and examined so there are no sharp edges and that any body parts don't get caught. Finally, don't use anything breakable.

Here we go!

Food-based Enrichment

Be sure to check the breeder's section regarding food and feeding. However, there are a number of new places and ways that you can feed your puppy listed on the Owner's Checklist. And you can combine them – for example, from a food dispensing toy under the dining room table near your cat or from a steel dish in the living room in the middle of the room when he is alone.

- Hide food in boxes of all shapes and sizes.
- Stuff carrots in sterilized long marrow bones.
- Cut tennis balls in half, put treats and/or food in a cupcake tray, and then put the tennis balls on top, so your puppy has to flip the tennis balls off to get to the treat.
- Fill cardboard takeout containers with kibble, treats, and water or broth and freeze. (Take off metal handle.)
- Put his food in food dispensing puzzle toys. My favorites are the Nina Ottosson toys.
- Freeze marrow bones or stuffed Kongs.
- Get a large cardboard box and cut out portions of it as doorways. Put treats inside, so your puppy has to go inside to get the treats – or he can just hang out (literally as you can see by this photo!).

(Photo courtesy of Meir Bartur)

- Hide treats and kibble so your dog can find them.
- Fill a sterilized bone or Kong with unsalted, no-sugar peanut butter.
- Put moist dog food on chew toys or inside Kongs and freeze them.
- Open a paper grocery bag on the floor and toss food inside.
- Poke holes in a plastic milk or water bottle and put treats and kibble inside. Take the cap off so he does not swallow it.
- Put a smelly treat in a small cardboard box which you put in a larger box which you put in a paper bag which you put in a larger box, etc. so that there are layers that your puppy has to get through to get the treat.
- Put treats and/or kibble inside cardboard toilet paper or paper towel rolls and close the ends, so he has to open it to get the food out.
- Put treats and/or kibble inside a tissue box.
- Scatter food and/or treats on the floor and then put a bed sheet or towel over it so he has to move it to find them.

Sometimes people are uncomfortable about scattering the food because they think it's mean or they don't want their puppy to eat on the rug in the living room or they think it's messy. Well, only scatter dry food! And feeding him like this is not going to be forever. Plus, remember why we're doing this – so he can make the connections between his brain cells. If you do not want him to eat on your rug in the living room, then scatter the food on your kitchen floor. It's not messy because he's going to be hungry and eat it!

- Scatter plastic bottles and containers with treats or kibble on the floor, so he has to get the food out.

Sensory Enrichment

- Cushions on the sofa? Take them off. Or stack them up.
- Drawers in the cabinet? Instead of keeping them closed, leave them partially open. Take one out, empty it, and turn it upside down on the floor.
- Chairs around your dining room table? Boy, there's a lot you can do with those.
  - o Move some chairs away from the table.
  - o Move all of them away from the table.
  - o Put some chairs on top of the table upside down.
  - o Put some chairs on top of the table right side up.
  - o Move the table back and line the chairs up in the middle of the dining room.
  - o Stack some chairs on top of each other.
  - o Line them up back to back and put a bed sheet over them so now he has a tunnel that he can run through.
  - o Tip one or more chairs on their sides.
  - o Place the top of the chair forward on the ground, so it makes a tunnel between the seat and the top.

- Guide him through legs of chairs.
- Hang some clothes on doorknobs or on the top corner of drawers.
- Hang things from a door frame or ceiling to tug on.
- Leave cabinet doors open so he can explore inside. (Take all breakables and spillables out.)
- Put lots of toys, baskets, and cartons in a pile in the middle of the floor so he has to pull one out to get it.
- Spread toys, baskets, and cartons across the floor, so he has to maneuver around them.
- Make an obstacle course out of your hallway by populating it with a broom that he has to hop over, a chair on its side, a folded up clothes dryer, an overturned drawer, etc.

- Move things out of their normal places in your home – move the couch to where the chair is and the chair to where the end table is, for example.
- Put plastic containers of all shapes and sizes and their lids on the ground as obstacles.
- Put a sheet over your sofa so it looks different.
- Put a squeaky toy inside of a paper bag.
- Put a towel on the back of a chair.
- Put a trash can on its side and throw a toy inside.

Social Enrichment

- Invite some puppies and dogs over for a puppy party. Make sure they are healthy, vaccinated, and like puppies.
- Invite some people over for a puppy party. Make sure they are healthy and vaccinated – just kidding!

Novel Items

- Give him different toys of different textures to play with.
- Put a laundry basket on its side for him to go in and out.
- Put a tarp down so your puppy has to walk over it to get to a toy in the center of the tarp.
- Open an umbrella so he gets used to hearing it and seeing it.
- Get a small step stool for him to climb on or over when he goes through a doorway. Block the doorway so stepping over it is the only way he can get through.
- Spread traffic cones over the floor and guide him through.
- Put towels on floor, so the floor looks different.
- Get a children's tunnel for him to run through.

- Get a Wobble board for him to learn to balance on.
- Secure wood planks on cinder blocks so he can walk up and down.

You may purchase most of these products at http://dogbookslibrary.com/breeding-whelping-genetics.php, http://www.dogbookslibrary.com/agility.php#Products, and http://www.dogbookslibrary.com/puppies.php#Products where I have handpicked everything on that site.

Do the exercises described above both when your puppy is in the room with you so he can see you moving things around, and then change the room when he cannot see you so he comes in to a totally new room.

One huge caveat – some people think they are giving their puppies exercise if they take a laser/flashlight and have him follow it on the floor. Personally, I would never do this. You can inadvertently direct the laser beam into your puppy's eyes, which can cause eye damage or cause them to develop an obsessive behavior disorder.

> **True story** – Lasers trigger the chase instinct, and the beam can never be caught. Many dogs transfer these chasing instincts from the laser beam to shadows and lights. One client had to take her watch off the instant she came home just in case the light hit the watch dial and reflected on the walls or floors, which would set her dog off on the chase, knocking down furniture in the process. The saddest part was that it was not her fault – her neighbor was dog sitting one day while it was raining. The neighbor could not walk the dog, so she thought she could exercise him inside with the laser similar to the way she exercised her cats. All it took was this one instance, and the

dog became obsessed with lights and shadows. Very sad.

Obedience Training

Start training some simple obedience exercises, such as Sit. You can do this even if you're watching TV – training sessions need to be short because of his short attention span, so you can train during commercials. While you are watching the program, keep him occupied with something to chew on while he is in his bed on the floor.

Exercises to Do Outside Your Home

There are four major areas to introduce your puppy to outside your house:

- The Environment
- The Car
- People
- Dogs

The Environment

Your Yard

If you live in a house with a yard, then start there. Your yard is probably similar to the inside of your house in that physically, it doesn't change much. But your yard has the wind to enrich it with new smells and critters that fly and scurry around, so being outside is much more stimulating to your puppy than being inside, so much so that many puppies and dogs do not like to come inside the house!

(Photo courtesy of Meir Bartur)

You can also set up new experiences for your puppy outside (and he'll find things on his own):

- Large boxes that you can cut doors in to use as tunnels
- Floating toys, frozen treats, or ice cubes in a wading pool that he can go diving for
- Exploring a coiled-up hose (Betcha never knew that was an obstacle course!)

(Photo courtesy of Meir Bartur)

- Wading pool without water full of balls that he has to move to find treats

PLEASE NOTE: When your puppy is in water, even if he is having the time of his life, take frequent breaks and limit his time to no more than five minutes in the water because he can swallow too much water and drown.

- Wading pool partly filled with water that he can splash in
- Wading pool with water with balls and toys
- Wading pool filled with sand that you bury toys in
- Old wooden cable spool or hose caddy to explore
- Things hanging from trees such as an old tire, some on bungee cords low enough that he can tug
- Large plastic trash can turned on its side. Your puppy can go inside, and it also moves.
- Old tires – car and bicycle – to crawl in and out of
- Motorized toys to chase

Outside your Yard

Several years ago, I was looking through a catalogue for dog supplies and burst out laughing because there was a puppy stroller! How ridiculous. Now I don't think it's so ridiculous. In fact, it's my favorite thing to introduce your puppy to many things safely.

Why? Not only can you take him outside to experience the sights and sounds firsthand, but remember that his primary sense is the sense of smell – and he can smell so many more things than we can. If we smell stew cooking on the stove, that's what we smell, stew. But our dogs smell each aroma of the meat, carrots, potatoes, and spices individually. So when you walk him, he is familiarizing himself with the smells of outdoors, which are very different from the smells of indoors.

Movement is something else he gets used to by riding in the stroller. Some dogs are afraid of cars because the movement affects their balance. Being in a stroller may minimize his fear of cars because he has felt movement in the stroller, which can transfer to movement in the car.

Veterinarians tell you not to take your puppy outside because his feet touch the ground, and the ground is where he can pick up diseases from other dogs' excrement – as well as eat things that are not good for him. If he's in a stroller, then his feet are not touching the ground – and he cannot eat anything he's not supposed to!

Depending on the size of your puppy, you can use:

- A granny shopping cart
- A puppy carrier (or sling), which you can use if you're just going out for a quick chore such as making a bank deposit or dropping off your clothes at the dry cleaner's
- A shopping cart
- A soft-sided kennel (Be careful here because your puppy could chew through it.)
- An old baby carriage or stroller
- A wagon
- Your dog's crate in a wagon
- Your dog's crate on a dog crate dolly (used in dog shows)
- Your dog's crate on a regular dolly (I'd use this as a last resort because the crate is at an angle rather than lying flat.)
- Your dog's crate on a skateboard

If whatever you're using is open, such a wagon, put something over the top to prevent him from jumping out and/or secure him inside. Put a towel or his bed in the bottom and give him some toys to play with. (I happen to be lazy, and that's why I would buy a stroller.)

Many employers permit their employees to bring their dogs to work. Hats off to your employer if you work in a place like that! Make sure your puppy is potty trained, and make sure that other dogs are friendly and welcome an addition into their turf. If you cannot watch your puppy because you are busy, then keep him around your desk area either by gating him in your office or cubicle, crating him, or using an Xpen. Your puppy is your responsibility. Although your co-workers may look out for him, no one is going to have as much commitment as you do. Don't let him wander around the office or even your cubicle if your eyes are not on him 100% of the time. There are way too many temptations for him – such as an incredible number of computer cords. One chomp, and.........

Take him to stores or other outdoor venues. Before taking your puppy out to stores, be sure to find out whether they will allow you to bring your puppy inside. Potty him first, and bring clean-up supplies, just in case.

Here's just a smattering of places to go:

- Banks
- Bicycle shops
- Christmas tree shopping
- Craft stores
- Department stores
- Home improvement stores
- Music stores
- Open air marketplaces and craft fairs
- Outdoor cafes, restaurants, and coffee houses

- Pumpkin patch shopping
- Schools
- Shopping and outlet centers
- Sport venues such as soccer fields
- Sporting good stores
- Wharfs and piers
- Wineries

And one final note regarding the environment. If you ultimately would like your dog to toilet outside on the grass but can't take him out because of the weather or his or your incapacity, then I highly recommend Fresh Patch, which is hydroponically grown grass that comes delivered to your door in a box similar to a pizza box. I like this product because it is real grass and because it is easy to set up, to use, and dispose of – all you have to do is open the box and then simply throw it out in the trash! You do need to pick up the poop, but there is no tray for the pee to slosh around in while you are carrying it to the toilet, in other words, nothing else to clean.

The Car

The car is one of the first places your puppy should be comfortable. He may have a dislike for the car because bad things happened there in his past:

- He was taken away from his mom and littermates in a car.
- He was taken in a car to a vet who hurt him by giving him shots.
- He was taken in a car to a groomer who poked and prodded him.
- His first rides were on a winding road, so he got carsick.

So change the association with the car and take him to some fun places.

- Bring a favorite toy or his bed (I like the ones with sides.) so he has something familiar in the car.
- You can take him for a short ride in the crate while he is napping.
- Stop the car frequently and let him look at the world outside.

Safety first!

- Use a doggie seatbelt.
- Put him in a crate and secure the crate with a seatbelt.
- Open the windows only three inches – please do not open them all the way or even further than three inches because he can fall out, especially if you stop suddenly.
- Lock electric windows – so if your puppy reaches them, he does not accidentally move them up or down.

> **True story** – I have seen dogs fall out of car windows and the back of a truck. I was on the freeway and saw a puppy crawling around on the open back of a slat bed truck. I watched in horror as he fell off the back and rolled to the side of the road. Both I and a highway patrol officer were able to stop the driver, who told us that he had just picked up the puppy (at seven weeks) and wanted to teach him to ride in the back of the truck because someone had told him to start training the instant he got the puppy. Dumb. Really dumb.

He may either be afraid of the car or get carsick – or both.

If he is afraid:

- If he's afraid of the car, then begin feeding his meals in the car while it is stopped – and don't take him for a ride for four hours after eating because he can get carsick.
- Use Adaptil (which is a calming pheromone), Chill-Out spray (which is a lavender, marjoram, and chamomile spray), Through a Dog's Ear (which is a calming CD)
- You can use your car as an obstacle course. Open all the doors. Have your dog on leash, and climb in and out of the car, going in and out of all the doors. Take a break, repeat a couple more times, and then do the same thing with the engine running.
- Open the back seat passenger doors of the car. You stand on one side and someone else has your puppy on the other side, and you call him to you and give him a scrumptious treat when he gets to you.
- If he's afraid of large trucks or noises such as motorcycles, put the crate on the floor or if it's on the seat, have a passenger feed him a scrumptious treat as soon as *you* hear it. Don't wait until it's passing right next to you. Also play traffic noise CDs in the house at various times during the day.

If he gets carsick:

- Make sure he has an empty stomach and don't feed him for at least four hours before the ride. If he still is a little queasy, there are several things you can do:
  o Give him a ginger snap before the ride.
  o Put him in his crate and strap the crate in with the seatbelt, or get a booster seat where he is strapped in.
  o Put the crate on the floor.

- If it's a plastic crate, put it upside down with the windows at the bottom. If it's wire, put a cloth over the top.

NEVER leave your puppy alone in the car whether he is in a crate or not.

True story – One of my clients dashed into Target for just five minutes and left her puppy in a crate that was on the floor. It was a cool day, but she wanted to be careful "just in case" and left the windows open an inch. She was in the store for less than ten minutes. When she returned, her car had been broken into and her puppy was stolen. Because of this incident, I wrote an article on Finding Stolen Dogs, which you can find here http://www.doggiemanners.com/art_finding_stolen_dogs.html .

People

Outside your house the biggest issue you'll encounter is well-meaning people, some of whom have no respect for your or your puppy's personal space. You are his advocate, and it is up to you to be in charge and keep him safe. If you have a three-month-old baby and a perfect stranger comes up to him and wants to hug him, what would you do? I doubt that you would hand him over to "socialize" him so he is good with strangers. How would you like it if that person picked him up out of his stroller or took him from your arms? Why can't we treat dogs with the same caution and respect as we treat babies? I'm getting off my soapbox now.

There are two categories of people – adults and children. Under each of these categories are many, many, many subcategories – a tall man with a beard is a different category than a woman wearing a hat and carrying an umbrella. A five-year-old little girl who is sitting next to your puppy petting him is very different from an eight-year-old boy poking him. A two-week-old baby being held by a person is very different from a two-year-old toddler running around the house.

How do you want your puppy to act around people?

There are two schools of thought regarding this, and I apologize in advance to anyone that is offended because this is contrary to what many trainers say, and that certainly is not my purpose. My purpose is to let you know what over 20 years of training has taught me, so you won't get into trouble.

One school is that your puppy should go up and greet every dog, every person, every new thing on the planet. The other is to look to you for guidance. Yes, it's rewarding to you to see your puppy being a social butterfly and being well liked, but I personally prefer the second method for several reasons:

- If other dogs and people pay attention to your dog, then he is being rewarded by them and not by you. Then if he gets too exuberant, you generally will hold him back. How that translates down the line is that everything in the environment is rewarding to your dog, and *you* become the bad guy! "They are novel, they pay attention to me, AND they give me treats. YOU are boring and keep telling me what to do and putting boundaries on me. Therefore, I choose other people over you." That's a sure-fire recipe of training your dog not to listen to you and never to come to you when you call him.

- Still another issue is that many people are just plain rude and don't respect your or the puppy's personal space – and the ones who are the most egregious are the ones that tell you, "You don't have to train him around me. All dogs like me." They will not ask if he's shy or timid and may handle him roughly. They do not understand dog body language to tell if he is stressed or afraid. He's scared, so he bites. Perfectly acceptable dog behavior because he does not like that type of handling – but one that can cause you a lawsuit.

- Others want to express affection, so they hug and kiss. Hugging is threatening to dogs, even though they *may* tolerate hugs from their owners. But not from strangers. And kissing, wow, now the stranger has her face right next to your puppy's face. Yikes, that's yet another bite waiting to happen! How would you like it if a perfect stranger came up to your child and tried to kiss him in the face?

- Or maybe he will overcome his fear of strangers by having them give him treats. That *may* happen. But what also can happen is that it can lull both of you into a false sense of security because he may be okay with that person in that one place at that specific time. It may not carry over to the next person, especially if that person does not have a treat. Now your puppy and the person are right next to each other – he's been taught to go to a stranger to get a treat. The only reason he came to the person was to get a treat. *This* person does not have a treat; he still is afraid, so what's stopping him from biting the person?

- But he comes to get a treat and retreats. Now he's eaten the food, he still is afraid and so he barks. The person backs up. Now he has learned that barking makes strangers go away.

It's a lot easier to prevent the problem from happening than to deal with it afterwards. It's your prerogative to let a person interact with your puppy or not. Just say no. Don't let anyone jeopardize your relationship with your puppy, especially if this occurs during his fear period. Some of this may sound unkind, but your puppy's welfare is important.

Tell people to ignore your puppy unless and until you want them to interact with him, and then tell them specifically what you want them to do or not do:

- Don't invade his space.
- Don't loom over him (which can be very scary).
- Don't talk to him.
- Don't hug him.
- And for heaven's sake, don't pet him until you give her specific directions – then tell her exactly how to do it. Put him on the ground if you are holding him because it's too tempting for her to try to kiss him if he's in your arms, and it gives him the option to interact or not. (Again, you will have to decide whether it is safe for his feet to touch the ground.)
  - o When he's on the ground, let him approach her rather than her coming towards him.
  - o Don't reach over his head to pet him.
  - o Kneel down and turn sideways.
  - o Relax the head and shoulders.
  - o Put her weight on her back foot.
  - o Look at him with soft eyes.
  - o Talk to him in a happy voice calmly.
  - o Let him smell her hand and decide whether he wants further contact.
  - o If he does, then she should scratch him under his chin or on his chest. If he does not engage, stop.
  - o Do not let her give him treats or pick him up.

Adults

Keeping all this in mind, let's start with adults first. Just as when you get behind the wheel of your car, you are engaging in defensive driving where you anticipate dangerous situations, defensive puppy handling is when you do your best to anticipate all the ridiculous things that people will do to your puppy.

Remember that you are your puppy's advocate. He trusts you to keep him safe since you are his leader. I'm trying to say this as politically correct as I can, but some people have no clue as to how a puppy feels when they are interacting with him because they are in their own world satisfying their own needs. So, it's up to you to protect your puppy and carefully orchestrate how they interact with him. It's much safer for both of you in the long run to have people become part of the background rather than have them stand out as something to play with.

Let's talk for a minute about how we greet people and how dogs greet other dogs. It's considered polite when we greet another person to face them and extend our hand so we can shake their hand. With dogs, this face-to-face meeting is a considered a threat – plus there is this strange hand coming towards them. How does your puppy know that this hand is friend or foe?   He does not know this person. Is the hand going to hurt him or snatch him away? Plus some stranger stares at him and show her teeth (even though she is smiling), both of which are threats in dogdom.

Since many people will not listen to you or don't hear what you are saying, the easiest way to stop them is to block them – put your arm out and give them a "stop signal" (extending your arm, palm facing them) or turning away from them. At the same time, tell them that you are training your puppy. If they still do not stop, then tell them to back off. Don't be afraid that you will hurt their feelings. Someone who really is a "dog person" thinks more about the welfare of the dog than their own gratification. They may be acting instinctively because your puppy is taking her back to a wonderful childhood memory, or they are simply rude for invading both your and your puppy's space. You are going to live with this puppy for several years, and these people is going to be out of your life in a New York minute and you probably will not see them ever again. Which relationship is more important to you?

My preferred method when your puppy meets a new person is to have him look at you for a treat, petting, or praise, especially or if he seems hesitant. If you want him to engage, since you have control over yourself and not the other person, you can approach and retreat as many times as necessary, each time getting a little closer as he feels more comfortable.

Alternatively, you can teach him to Target if you think he may be fearful. (See Appendix 7 on Targeting.) You need to train this *before* he encounters the scary stuff. You cannot train during a crisis! Remember a few years ago when the plane crashed on the Hudson River? Captain Sullenberger did not pull out the handbook to Page 33 to see what to do as his plane was crashing into the river. He had practiced on a flight simulator numerous times before the actual crash so each step became muscle memory. So both you and your puppy need to know what to do before the "crash" to teach him to look to you for leadership. Additionally, targeting is useful for many more things than just overcoming fears, so it is a good behavior to teach.

Children

Now we come to people even scarier (gasp) to puppies – children. It's not just small children but also older ones –

young children run around, older children don't know their own strength when handling a puppy, and teenagers like to provoke.

If you have children at home and he is comfortable around them, that does not necessarily translate to other children. Can you imagine from your puppy's point of view how he views other children as unpredictable scary aliens running around, flailing their arms in the air, and screaming? And then one of them comes up to him, picks him up, and hugs him. Again, he does what a normal puppy would do – bite at the scary thing to make it go away. The closest body part is the face, so the child gets bitten in the face. Lawyers love lawsuits where dogs bite children because they are pretty much a slam dunk for a big payoff for the bitee.

Hopefully your breeder has introduced your puppy to children. If not, then you need to do this, pronto. At least get him used to rough handling from you before he encounters it from a stranger. If he has never been handled roughly by the people whom he knows best and then gets knocked around by a little kid, this sets him up not to have a good association with children for the rest of his life. Go to the Checklist and start doing the handling exercises ASAP and also to Appendix 5 for Hand Shyness exercises.

Teach your children how to interact safely with the puppy. With small children especially, they have to be seated and to be still before you put the puppy in their lap. Then you tell them exactly how to pet them – from the back of the neck to the tail or from the chin down to his chest, petting in the direction that the hair grows. And it's soft petting, no poking, pinching, hitting, lying on top, hugging, etc.

Let your puppy determine whether he is having fun – and this test holds true for any experience, not just with children. Stop interacting and see if the puppy wants to continue. If he is wagging his tail and tries to interact, then continue. If his tail is between his legs, he is shaking or holds still, or if he tries to run away and hide, stop and try to determine why he does not like what's going on. (Refer to Appendix 6 on Fear for more information.) Give everyone a chance to compose themselves, and then try again at a lower intensity. If he still is uncomfortable, then stop and call a trainer to help guide you.

I also encourage neighborhood children to come and meet your puppy because if your dog is in your yard, neighborhood kids are less likely to tease a dog that they know.

How should children interact with your puppy? If there is a group of children that comes up and wants to pet your puppy, the same rules for grown-ups and your children apply, but there are some additional ones:

- One child can interact at a time.
- No hugging, no kissing.
- No jumping around, no waving your arms.
- Respect his space.
- Stop if the puppy wants to stop. If you see any signs that he is nervous, then stop immediately. That's a huge point – YOU need to be there every second to stop things before they start.

This book is about socializing your puppy, not about teaching children how to behave around dogs. But I do have an article on one of my websites about children and dogs here http://www.DoggieManners.com/art_dogs_and_children.html and also recommend some excellent books.

Dogs

Meeting dogs cannot be "chance encounters." You need to be in charge and carefully orchestrate them because your puppy forms either good or bad associations from these meetings. Even though a person says her dog is friendly, if your puppy greets him with over-the-top enthusiasm, then the dog may correct him by snapping and/or biting him – or scaring him when he cannot run away. I can't tell you how many times I've heard, "Well, he's never done *that* before." The result – your puppy could develop fears of that type of dog or dogs in general for the rest of his life.

If your puppy is paying attention to other dogs and then gets excited, you likely will try to make him calm down. Once again, *you* become the bad guy and you're training your puppy never to pay attention to you around other dogs because you always take him away from good doggie stuff. He may interact if you want him to, but he has to make eye contact with you and get permission first.

So, first, look for a safe puppy to interact with yours.

What does "safe" mean? A dog who:
- Has a negative fecal test
- Is healthy with no diseases
- Is friendly
- Is not a bully – meaning he wants to play rougher, differently, or more intensely than your puppy does or will not stop playing when your puppy wants to. If that happens, you need to stop play immediately for a time-out. Don't yell at the other puppy; just separate them so they can calm down. Resume playing to see if the lesson was learned. If it was not, then stop play with that puppy and find another one for yours to play with.

- Likes to play with puppies
- Is vaccinated

Sometimes play looks like it is really rough. But if both dogs are having fun, then let it continue. How can you tell if it's fun?

- Both puppies change positions. If they are wrestling, one switches from one being on the top to the bottom. If they are chasing each other, one switches from the chaser to the chasee.
- If they self-regulate, meaning they stop for a nanosecond to regroup and then both want to play again.
- If they stop and neither is slinking away or trying to hide.

If someone has two puppies and wants them to play with yours, let them play one at a time so they do not gang up on your puppy. If your puppy accepts both of them, then they can all play together unless they start to gang up.

Then find an adult dog who is not aggressive and will not hurt your puppy but who will not hesitate to tell him that his behavior is not appropriate. This is a huge lesson. Keep in mind that some dogs are territorial about their own turf, so meet on neutral territory or in your house.

> **True Story** – I took my dogs to the park every day for several years. Chadwick, who is the mascot on my Doggie Manners website (aside from being the cutest dog in the world!), weighed about 55 pounds and had no interest in playing with other dogs other than my two dogs. But he was like a magnet to puppies, and they would pester him to play because his long blond hair was easily seen and blew in the wind. They would jump on him. He would show his teeth. They

would jump on him again. He would show his teeth and growl. They would jump on him a third time, and he would nail them – never hurting them but telling them in no uncertain terms after two warnings that he wanted to be left alone. He had a reputation as a puppy hater.

I was very concerned at the time because I did not know as much about dog behavior as I do now. So I asked several well-known trainers and behaviorists about it, and they all asked me the same question, "He gives them warnings; he never hurts any of the puppies; right? Then you should be charging their owners for the valuable lesson he's teaching them."

You need to find a dog like Chadwick!

Chapter 9

Checklist for Owners

If you would like a hard copy of the
Owner's Checklist so you can
actually check items off,
please email me at
caryl@PuppySocializationGuide.com.

Remember that socializing is interacting, and your puppy cannot socialize with a bench at a bus stop. Your goal is to familiarize your puppy and make him comfortable with and around as many of these situations as you can. Notice your puppy's reaction. The best reaction is to ignore or accept each circumstance. If he's okay with something new, then go on to the next thing. If he is not, then refer to the appendix for strategies and training methods to help him. And make sure those associations are good for him.

An easy way to do this is to bring him along during your daily routines – take him with you when you go to the bank, drive your kids to school, go to the dry cleaners, etc. But **think ahead** – if you know you will be going to a grocery store or restaurant where dogs are not allowed, do not leave him in the car or tie him up outside.

By taking him with you, you introduce him to new sights, sounds, and locations – and smells. But you do not know what smells you're introducing him to because his sense of smell is so much greater than ours. Plus there are hundreds of smells on each walk, so he is bombarded with sensory stimuli. And his sense of smell is directly connected to his primitive brain, and the associations with the primitive brain are very powerful.

> **True story** – One of my clients wants her four-month-old Golden Retriever to be a service dog. We had two lessons, and then we could not meet for three weeks. At our second lesson, we worked on loose-leash walking because he was either pulling her in every direction or stopping and sitting, both of which are typical puppy behaviors. During our break, she took her puppy everywhere.
>
> For our third lesson, we met at a park, and that dog was so self assured and composed that I could not believe he was only four months old! Yes, his "goofy puppiness" popped out occasionally, but he was mature far beyond his chronological age. He observed the world around him but was focused on her. This is an excellent beginning to his training.

A week after your puppy has had his last puppy shot, begin to take him to the same places that you did when he was in a carrier – but now he is walking and on a leash, so it is a different experience for him. It is possible that he may be frightened. If he is, then refer to appendices 6 and 7 on Fears and Targeting.

Try not to overwhelm him. Again, notice his reaction. If he seems unsure, then wait for him to figure it out – patience is a virtue. An alternative to giving him a treat in this situation is to have him Sit to get his mind on something else. Or you can bring a ball or squeaky toy along to bounce or squeak.

Here's the list:

Awakening

By a door slamming
By being touched

By someone walking by
By stamping your feet

With different sounds (alarm, clapping, radio music, door slamming, etc.)

Being touched or held (Handle each body part – give him a treat.)

Bathing
Brushing
Clipping each nail
Examining each ear
Grabbing gently his skin
Holding his hips
Holding his shoulders
Hugging from behind
Hugging from the front
Hugging from the side
Lifting him onto your washing machine (It's similar to a vet exam table.)
Lifting onto a table
Moving his tongue
Near his anus
Near his genitals
On both sides of his body
On each foot
On each side of his neck
On his chest
On his groin
On his gums and teeth
On his head
On his legs (each leg)

On his mouth
On his neck
On his tail
On his tummy
Opening his mouth gently
Pinching his skin
Pressing gently on his spine
Restrained gently on back
Restrained gently on side
Restrained on a table
Restraining gently his body
Restraining gently his head
Rotating his legs
Squeezing gently each toe
Squeezing gently his feet
Squeezing gently his tail
Touching the roof of his mouth
Wearing a harness
Wearing a head halter
When he's on a table
When he's on each side
When he's on his back
When he's on the floor
When he's on your lap

Climbing

In a box
Out of a box
Over low obstacles
Up and down steps/stairs

Backless
Carpeted
Concrete
Curving
Dark
Inside
Lighted
Long
Metal
Narrow

Open slabs
Outside
Shallow
Short
Steep
Wide
With railings
Without railings
Wooden
Wooden and carpeted

Dogs

Size

Tiny
Small
Medium

Large
Giant
Long

Age

Puppy
Adolescent

Adult
Senior

Coat

Black
Blonde
Furry
Merle
Red

Slick coat
Spotted
Tan
White

Ears

Airplane
Back
Bat
Droopy
Flattened

Folded over
Forward
Prick or upright
Rounded tip

Tail

Bob
Bushy
Curled
Docked
Hanging naturally
Lower
None
Otter

Parallel to ground
Raised up
Ring
smooth
Stumpy
Tucked
Whip

Other

Barking
Behind a fence
Flat-faced dogs
Slinking
Staring
Wearing costume
Whining

Standing
Running
Sitting
Lying down
On leash
Off leash

Eating

At a friend's house
By scattering the food in every room
By scattering the food in your yard
In a corner
In food dispensing toys
In puzzle toys
In the back yard
In the basement
In the bathroom
In the bathtub
In the car
In the crate
In the dining room
In the front yard
In the kitchen
In the laundry room
In the living room
In the middle of the room
In the schoolyard
On concrete
On the countertop
On the grass
On your back porch
On your front porch
Under a table
Under an umbrella
When he is alone
When other people or animals are present.

Hearing

Airplanes
Baby crying
Buzzer
Cars backfiring
Cheering crowds
Clapping crowds
Children screaming
Crackling sounds
Crinkling sounds
Deep voices
Dishwasher
Doorbell
Echoes
Fax machine
Fireworks
Garbage truck
Hair dryer
Hedge trimmers
Hissing sounds
Intercom
Knocking at your door
Large truck
Lawnmower
Leaf blower
Loud music
Loudspeaker announcements
Motorcycle
Moving vans
Musical instruments
Noisy machinery
People applauding
People laughing
People shaking a towel
People shouting
People whispering
Phone ringing
Popping sounds
Pot lids dropping on the floor
Power tools
Printer
Shredder
Sirens
Skateboards
Snow blowers
Sprinklers
Squeaky voices
Street cleaning trucks
Sudden loud noise
Sudden scary noise
Thunder
Trains
Trucks
Trucks backing up
Vacuum cleaner
Washing machine
Weed cutters
Whistling tea kettle

Meeting

10 different babies
10 different toddlers
10 different puppies
10 different small pets
10 different birds
10 different cats
10 different men
10 different women

10 different young boys
10 different young girls
10 different ethnicities
10 different senior citizens
10 large friendly dogs
10 small friendly dogs
10 teenage boys
10 teenage girls

Playing with (Safety precautions apply.)

Buster-Cube
Kong
Havaball
Roll-a-ball
Chew toys
Frisbees
Hula hoops
Kongs
Balls of all kinds
Bones
Fabric

Flexible
Frisbee
Hard
Nubby surface
Nylon bones
Plastic
Rope toys
Smooth surface
Soft
Squeaky
Tug toys

Sleeping in or on

Bathroom
Car
Crates or kennels of all types
Den
Dining room
Everyone's bedroom
Kitchen
Laundry room

Living room
Someone else's house
Someone's lap

In all these places in a crate, rug, bare floor

Seeing People

Dressed in costumes and masks
Dressed unusually (such as a woman in a billowing skirt or dress)
Of all ages and sexes

Homeless people
In a cast
In uniforms
Of different races and ethnic origins

Engaged in these activities

Collecting cans from dumpsters
Dancing
Lying on the ground
Moving their arms quickly
Pushing a wheelchair
Raising their arms above their head
Riding in a wheelchair
Shouting
Sitting on benches
Walking with a strange gait or limp
Waving something
Who are drunk
Who are pulling a wagon
Who walk erratically
With baby carriages
With backpacks
With dogs
With other animals
With rapid movement
With slow cautious movement
With spasmodic movement

Carrying and/or using

Backpacks
Brooms
Camera
Construction tools such as a hammer
Gardening equipment
Golf clubs
Groceries
Hose
Knapsacks
Large and small packages
Luggage
Mops
Power tools
Shopping carts
Shovels
Tennis rackets
Umbrellas opened and closed
Wheelbarrows

Moving by

Bicycling
Dancing
Exercising
Jogging
Roller blading
Running
Scooters
Skateboarding
Skating both ice skates and roller skates
Skipping
Swimming
Using a cane
Using a walker
Walking on crutches
Wheelchair both electric and manual

Playing

Baseball
Basketball
Children playing games
Football
Golf
Jump rope
Kites
Soccer
Table tennis
Tennis
Volleyball

Sitting on

Chairs
Ground
Park benches
Rocking chairs
Sofas
Wheelchairs

Throwing/playing with
> Remote controlled toys
>
> Squeaky toys
>
> Sticks

> Tug toys
>
> Toys

Wearing
> Baseball caps
> Boots
> Bulky coats
> Glasses
> Gloves
> Hats
> Hoodies

> Helmets
> Masks
> Nose rings
> Raincoats
> Silly costumes
> Sunglasses
> Trench coats

Working with
> Construction tools
> Hedge trimmers
> Lawn mowers
> Leaf blowers

> Pool cleaning tools
> Snow blowers and shovels
> Sports gear

Seeing other things

Airplanes
Bags of garbage
Balloons
Big stuffed animals
Blimps
Bubbles
Bus or train stops or stations
Cardboard boxes of all sizes
Ceiling fans both on and off
Closed spaces with people present
Closed spaces with no people present
Chairs upside down
Fire hydrants
Flapping cloths, awnings, flags

Furniture moved from its usual place
Garage doors opening and closing
Heavy equipment – being used and not used
Helicopters
Mirrors – on the floor, on the wall
People appearing out of nowhere
Plastic bags on the ground
Statues
Street vendors
Things floating in a fountain
Traffic
> At daytime
> At dusk
> At night
> Behind you
> Coming towards you
> Fast
> Heavy
>
> Light
> Slow

Trash cans on the street
Wide open spaces with people present
Wide open spaces with no people present
Your changing a light bulb
Your setting up the ironing board

Visiting

10 different houses
Airports
Auto shops
Banks
Baseball diamond
Basketball court
Beaches (dogs permitted)
Bookstores
Busy streets
Concert sites
Construction sites
Crowded places
Countryside
Drive-thrus
Dry cleaners
Elevators
Escalators
Farm or ranch
Farmer's markets
Fire station
Flea markets
Freeways
Garage

Gasoline stations
Groomer's shop
Hardware store
Kennel
Outdoor restaurant, coffee shop,
or ice cream parlor
Park
Pet store
Playgrounds
Police station
Printer
Quiet country locations
Riding in a car
Santa Claus
Shopping centers or malls
Soccer field
Street fairs
Tennis court
Vacuum cleaner stores
Vet's office
Video store
Yard sales
Your work site

Walking

Around objects
At the beach
Between objects
Between parked cars
In rain
In wind
In a creek
In the city
In the country
In a parking lot
In the suburbs

In a rural area
Over an A-frame
Over a bridge
Through a tunnel
Through a crowd of people
Under furniture
Under high obstacles

Walking on

Asphalt
Astroturf
Beach sand
Bubble wrap
Carpet
Concrete
Dirt
Grass

> Freshly mowed grass
> Wet grass
> When it's icy
> When it's raining
> When it's snowing

Grates in sidewalk or street
Gravel
Ice
Linoleum
Manhole covers
Metal
Mirror
Mud (sorry, but it's necessary!)
Mulch
Scale at vet's office
Slippery surfaces
Snow
Stairs
Tarp
Tile
Under a chair or table
Up and down a ramp
Vinyl
Wet concrete (rain wet, not newly poured!)
Wooden deck
Wood floors in your house

Remember that your job is to help your puppy get used to new situations, locations, sounds, sights, smells, and experiences now in a positive way so that he has a broad database to draw from when he is an adult. Have fun!

Chapter 10

A Word about Puppy Classes

We've talked about puppy classes previously. They can either be the best thing for your puppy or the worst. They can help shy puppies as well as bold puppies. It depends on how they are run, what the curriculum is, and the competence of the instructor.

There are very, very different curricula for these classes:

- One class may be puppies playing and running around together.
- Another may be an obedience class for puppies where there is no time to play.
- Another may be a puppy agility course.
- And yet another may be a combination of one or more of the above.

Every trainer has his or her own style of teaching classes as well as differing health and age requirements for the classes. It's essential that you research what the curriculum of the class is and then visit the class beforehand so you can be comfortable with the instructor, what is being taught, and how it is being taught.

Make sure that the instructor has at least ten years of experience! I have heard of obedience clubs and training businesses putting their newest instructor in charge of their puppy classes. This is the most important time in your puppy's life, and the person teaching should be well versed about puppies and puppy behavior, not simply potty training or playing with other puppies because "puppy issues" are different from adolescent or adult dog issues.

I think Puppy Kindergarten classes should cover very different issues than obedience classes. Why? Because your puppy can learn obedience exercises such as Sit, Down, Come, etc. at any time in his life. The two things that most puppy owners are concerned with are both ends of his body – the Front End dealing with chewing and mouthing as well as the Back End dealing with peeing and pooping. But think about what's going on *inside* his body – his developing brain – that needs to be addressed while he is still young.

As a trainer and behavior consultant, I am more concerned with socialization, familiarization, and handling exercises as well as confidence building because that all-important socialization window closes at 16 weeks. That's what I think puppy classes should be about. Others have different opinions. Again, just be sure you enroll your puppy in the right class *for your puppy* because puppy classes are vastly different.

I prefer puppy kindergarten classes that are more "pre-agility classes" focusing on equipment and working with the handler rather than "puppy obedience classes." By working together, puppies develop trust in their people and self confidence in themselves.

When your puppy is given positive experiences in a controlled setting, he becomes better adjusted in later life. His brain is developing, and the connections between the brain cells are increasing. The more connections and experiences he has, the better and broader his emotional and behavioral foundation.

Here's the description of my puppy classes, which reflects what I think is important.

My Puppy K classes are for puppies who:

- Are 10 to 16 weeks when they attend the first session
- Have at least two sets of vaccinations, the most recent being at least two days prior to starting class
- Are free of external and internal parasites (that means dewormed and no fleas!) Owners need to show proof of vaccination(s) and a recent fecal exam.
- Are in good health
- Have lived in your house at least two weeks (because if he has any medical conditions or diseases, they will likely become apparent within those two weeks)

The format each week is approximately the same – the puppies navigate one of two puppy agility courses (one deals with height and surface changes and movement, and the other is going through things). These are Confidence Building Exercises:

- Guiding your puppy through new experiences in a loving, gentle manner
- Going through our "puppy agility" course
- Helping your puppy get over his fears

Each week we have a lecture, and the topics rotate. During the lecture, inevitably puppies start to "act up," so I show owners how to deal with their behavior.

The lecture topics are:

- Socialization and Handling
  - Puppy developmental periods and what to look out for
  - Why socializing your puppy now is so important
  - How to socialize your puppy
  - Gentling exercises
  - How to handle your puppy
  - How to read your puppy's body language
  - Teaching him that new people aren't scary
  - Showing him that approaching hands are not scary
- Biting and Chewing
  - Why chewing and biting are important (Your puppy does need to do this!)
  - Appropriate puppy chew toys
  - Preventing you from becoming a human pin cushion
  - Learning the difference between what are his things and what things belong to other people
- Housetraining or potty training
  - How to prevent and help solve house training problems
  - The importance of routine
  - Predicting elimination and looking for signals
  - Praise when your puppy eliminates in the right place
  - Use of crates, X-pens, tethers
  - Proper clean-up products and procedures
  - Maintaining your sanity during training

- Obedience Training
  - What to say and how to say it
  - Why it's important to begin training now
  - Training your puppy to Sit
  - Training your puppy to Come to you

Finally, the puppies get to play with each other with supervised interaction while I narrate the play.

Interspersed at appropriate times during the classes, we discuss and have Leadership exercises:

- How to use your voice and body in training
- Why looking at your face is important for your puppy
- Teaching your puppy to respond to his name
- Giving your puppy boundaries and limits
- Puppy Zen (Teaching your puppy impulse control)
- The best games to play with your puppy

Again, those are the topics I think are important. I also give a written handout (soon to be a book – so wait for it!) so that my clients can have something concrete in their hands for review. Generally speaking, between the handout and the classes, my clients are satisfied. If there is an issue they need further help with, then we schedule a private lesson.

Chapter 11

Now What?

It would be really nice if your puppy were tied with a big red bow and be perfect! But that doesn't happen. Sigh. At five months, adolescence is beginning. That sweet little fur ball that you brought home just a few months ago now has raging hormones even if he has been neutered or she spayed. You were the center of his universe, but now you are b-o-r-i-n-g. He's familiar with you and your home. Absolutely *everything else* is more interesting than what he already knows and *HeHasToFindOutAboutThingsQuicklySinceThere'sNoTime ToSpare*!

It's likely that the time you spent training obedience and manners will fly out the window. Previously, when you told him to Sit, his rear end hit that ground pretty quickly. Now when you tell him to Sit, he looks around, sees if there is anything else that he wants to do, contemplates his navel, and then makes his decision whether to Sit or not.

I haven't counted how many phone calls I get that go something like, "I don't know what's happened to my puppy. Last week he was the sweetest thing. Now he won't listen. He pulls on the leash. He doesn't like to do X. He seems to be biting more – and now it *really* hurts. Sometimes he barks at the strangest things. He's defiant. One minute he's perfect, and the next he's a lunatic. What's going on?"

My reply is, "Welcome to adolescence! All that work that you did is still in his brain, but it's buried somewhere because finding out about new stuff is soooooo much more fun than rehashing the old stuff. It's a phase, and he will outgrow it.

"You're going to relate to him differently, much as you change the way you act around a toddler and a teenager. You need to continue to set boundaries and let him know that there are consequences for his actions. If you haven't begun obedience and manners training, don't put it off for a second longer. Literally, begin this instant so you can give him a framework on how to act – 'Sit while I put on your leash. Be quiet while I fix your dinner. Learn to keep all four feet on the ground rather than jump.'

"You need to speak the same language that he does and train in a way that he understands. Learn about how dogs learn, how dogs communicate, and dog body language. If I were speaking to you in Swedish, could you understand me? But most of all, remember that you and he are going to be together for a long time, so don't forget to have fun!"

RESCUE ORGANIZATIONS AND SHELTERS SECTION

Chapter 12

Socialization for Rescue Agencies and Shelters

While exposure to things in a positive light – such as socialization, habituation, and enrichment programs – are good for breeder's puppies, they are particularly important for shelter puppies, especially ones that are singletons or orphaned. There are many good shelter programs available on the Internet that also include training for adoption. These shelter and rescue programs offer more specific information on shelter and rescue dogs and facilities than I could offer here. You can integrate the information in this book along with those programs. However, I do think there are some unique opportunities for shelters and rescue agencies that most owners do not have.

Shelters and rescues have volunteers who come in to work with the dogs and puppies. These volunteers have set aside times in their days for interacting and training the puppies, as opposed to owners who have to squeeze in times during the day. There is a variety of people who can interact with the puppies in many different ways providing the puppies with many more exposure and familiarization opportunities to people as well as incorporating training. Shelters and rescuers can also move puppies to different foster homes to get them used to different sights, smells, sounds, etc.

Because shelters and rescue organizations generally are in a financial crunch, there are also inexpensive enrichment toys such as:

- Plastic water bottles, cardboard boxes, cardboard from paper towel rolls, or plastic containers where you can cut holes in them for treat dispensers.
- Put kibble in a plastic half-gallon milk container which you hang from the ceiling or from upper bars of the kennel.
- Freeze diluted chicken broth in plastic containers and give them as large ice cubes. (Spray with nonstick spray first to ease in emptying.)
- Crumpled pieces of paper with kibble or treats inside.
- Bags within boxes within boxes with kibble or treats.

Ask your supporters and dog toy manufacturers for donations of food dispensing toys. The Kong Company © donates its products, and you may register your organization here http://tinyurl.com/oq6p4tg.

Dr. Claudeen McAuliffe of the Humane Animal Welfare Society in Waukesha, WI has offered the following information from their Mod Squad™ Handbook on "Pup Squad:"

Pup Squad . . .

What is it? The Pup Squad program targets all puppies 5 months and under before their official evaluation. The critical period of socialization for puppies happens within their first 16 weeks and begins to taper off after this point. By 5 months, the window has closed significantly and the dog becomes fearful of things that it does not know or understand. A dog that missed out on socialization as a puppy may remain fearful of novel things, new people, new situations, etc. for the rest of its life. Behavior problems may result from this lack of early socialization. The Pup Squad program strives to provide socialization opportunities for puppies in the shelter during this critical period of socialization prior to evaluation.

How do pups enter the program? Puppies who are stray, surrendered or transferred from other shelters are eligible for the program. Shelter staff will notify **MOD SQUAD** ™ personnel when a puppy enters the shelter. An email will then be sent out to **MOD SQUAD** ™ members notifying everyone. Members can begin interactions with the puppy immediately.

How are dogs identified? The first person to work with the pup should be sure to do the following:

1. Hang an orange "Pup Squad" sign on the pup's kennel (if it is not already done by staff).

2. Enter a new page for the pup in the Pup Squad log.

3. Enter the pup's name on the dog log at a glance.

4. Fit puppy with a collar and harness and hang it on the puppy's kennel.

Who can interact with these pups? Only **MOD SQUAD** ™ volunteers work with these puppies. They will implement simple strategies concentrating on socialization, handling, environmental enrichment and the foundations for basic manners. Since each puppy will enter the program at various points of socialization, the program will strive to meet the puppy where it is in its development. Through positive experiences, the pup will progress at its own pace. After each session, the **MOD SQUAD** ™ member makes an entry in the Pup Squad log, summarizing the interaction.

Puppies who are not on the adoption floor, and not in the Infirmary, will be worked with in their kennels or other areas in the back of the shelter. These puppies are not yet available for adoption, so it will be important to keep them out of the public eye during adoption hours. Quiet areas in the non-public area of the shelter should be identified as possible working areas. When the weather permits, work can be done outdoors.

Puppies who are in the Infirmary should be worked with in areas where they will not contaminate healthy animals, but they MUST be worked with to minimize future behavior problems. Spaces should be designated for this purpose, and opportunities for enrichment and socialization should be provided.

Please be sure to check both the Breeder's Section and the Owner's Section of this book for more ideas.

APPENDIX

Appendix 1

I am very grateful to **Dr. Carmen Battaglia** for allowing me to use his article on www.BreedingBetterDogs.com on Early Neurological Stimulation.

Early Neurological Stimulation

Surprising as it may seem, it isn't capacity that explains the differences that exist between individuals because most seem to have far more capacity than they will ever use. The differences that exist between individuals seem to be related to something else. The ones who achieve and outperform others seem to have within themselves the ability to use hidden resources. In other words, it's what they are able to do with what they have that makes the difference.

In many animal breeding programs, the entire process of selection and management is founded on the belief that performance is inherited. Attempts to analyze the genetics of performance in a systematic way have involved some distinguished names such as Charles Darwin and Francis Galton. But it has only been in recent decades that good estimates of heritability of performance have been based on adequate data. Cunningham, (1991) in his study of horses, found that only by using Timeform data, and measuring groups of half brothers and half sisters could good estimates of performance be determined. His data shows that performance for speed is about 35% heritable. In other words, only about 35% of all the variation that is observed in track performance is controlled by heritable factors, the remaining 65% is attributable to other influences, such as training, management and nutrition. Cunningham's work while limited to horses, provides a good basis for understanding how much breeders can attribute to the genetics and the pedigrees.

Researchers have studied these phenomena and have looked for new ways to stimulate individuals in order to improve their natural abilities. Some of the methods discovered have produced life long lasting effects. Today many of the differences between individuals can now be explained by the use of early stimulation methods.

Introduction

Man for centuries has tried various methods to improve performance. Some of the methods have stood the test of time, others have not. Those who first conducted research on this topic believed that the period of early age was a most important time for stimulation because of its rapid growth and development. Today, we know that early life is a time when the physical immaturity of an organism is susceptible and responsive to a restricted but important class of stimuli. Because of its importance many studies have focused their efforts on the first few months of life.

Newborn pups are uniquely different from adults in several respects. When born, their eyes are closed and their digestive system has a limited capacity requiring periodic stimulation by their dam who routinely licks them in order to promote digestion. At this age they are only able to smell, suck, and crawl. Body temperature is maintained by snuggling close to their mother or by crawling into piles with other littermates. During these first few weeks of immobility, researchers noted that these immature and under-developed canines are sensitive to a restricted class of stimuli which includes thermal and tactile stimulation, motion and locomotion.

Other mammals such as mice and rats are also born with limitations, and they also have been found to demonstrate a similar sensitivity to the effects of early stimulation. Studies show that removing them from their nest for three minutes each day during the first five to ten days of life causes body temperatures to fall below normal. This mild form of stress is sufficient to stimulate hormonal, adrenal and pituitary systems. When tested later as adults, these same animals were better able to withstand stress than littermates who were not exposed to the same early stress exercises. As adults, they responded to stress in "a graded" fashion, while their non-stressed littermates responded in an "all or nothing way."

Data involving laboratory mice and rats also shows that stress in small amounts can produce adults who respond maximally. On the other hand, the results gathered from non-stressed littermate show that they become easily exhausted and are near death if exposed to intense prolonged stress. When tied down so they were unable to move for twenty-four hours, rats developed severe stomach ulcers, but littermates exposed to early stress handling were found to be more resistant to stress tests and did not show evidence of ulcers. A secondary affect was also noticed.

Sexual maturity was attained sooner in the littermates given early stress exercises. When tested for differences in health and disease, the stressed animals were found to be more resistant to certain forms of cancer and infectious diseases and could withstand terminal starvation and exposure to cold for longer periods than their non-stressed littermates.

Other studies involving early stimulation exercises have been successfully performed on both cats and dogs. In these studies, the Electrical Encephalogram (EEG) was found to be ideal for measuring the electrical activity in the brain because of its extreme sensitivity to changes in excitement, emotional stress, muscle tension, changes in oxygen and breathing. EEG measures show that pups and kittens when given early stimulation exercises mature at faster rates and perform better in certain problem solving tests than non-stimulated mates.

In the higher level animals the effect of early stimulation exercises have also been studied. The use of surrogate mothers and familiar objects were tested by both of the Kelloggs and Dr. Yearkes using young chimpanzees. Their pioneer research shows that the more primates were deprived of stimulation and interaction during early development, the less able they were to cope, adjust and later adapt to situations as adults.

While experiments have not yet produced specific information about the optimal amounts of stress needed to make young animals psychologically or physiologically superior, researchers agree that stress has value. What also is known is that a certain amount of stress for one may be too intense for another, and that too much stress can retard development. The results show that early stimulation exercises can have positive results but must be used with caution. In other words, too much stress can cause pathological adversities rather than physical or psychological superiority.

Methods of Stimulation

The U.S. Military in their canine program developed a method that still serves as a guide to what works. In an effort to improve the performance of dogs used for military purposes, a program called "Bio Sensor" was developed. Later, it became known to the public as the "Super Dog" Program. Based on years of research, the military learned that early neurological stimulation exercises could have important and lasting effects. Their studies confirmed that there are specific time periods early in life when neurological stimulation has optimum results. The first period involves a window of time that begins at the third day of life and lasts until the sixteenth day. It is believed that because this interval of time is a period of rapid neurological growth and development, and therefore is of great importance to the individual.

The "Bio Sensor" program was also concerned with early neurological stimulation in order to give the dog a superior advantage. Its development utilized six exercises which were designed to stimulate the neurological system. Each workout involved handling puppies once each day. The workouts required handling them one at a time while performing a series of five exercises. Listed in order of preference, the handler starts with one pup and stimulates it using each of the five exercises. The handler completes the series from beginning to end before starting with the next pup.

The handling of each pup once per day involves the following exercises:
1. Tactical stimulation (between toes)
2. Head held erect
3. Head pointed down
4. Supine position
5. Thermal stimulation.

Tactile stimulation

1. Tactile stimulation - holding the pup in one hand, the handler gently stimulates (tickles) the pup between the toes on any one foot using a Q-tip. It is not necessary to see that the pup is feeling the tickle. Time of stimulation 3 - 5 seconds. (Figure 1) [The illustrations are at the end of this Appendix.]

2. Head held erect - using both hands, the pup is held perpendicular to the ground, (straight up), so that its head is directly above its tail. This is an upwards position. Time of stimulation 3 - 5 seconds (Figure 2).

3. Head pointed down - holding the pup firmly with both hands the head is reversed and is pointed downward so that it is pointing towards the ground. Time of stimulation 3 - 5 seconds (Figure 3).

4. Supine position - hold the pup so that its back is resting in the palm of both hands with its muzzle facing the ceiling. The pup while on its back is allowed to sleep. Time of stimulation 3-5 seconds. (Figure 4)

5. Thermal stimulation—use a damp towel that has been cooled in a refrigerator for at least five minutes. Place the pup on the towel, feet down. Do not restrain it from moving. Time of stimulation 3-5 seconds. (Figure 5)

These five exercises will produce neurological stimulations, none of which naturally occur during this early period of life. Experience shows that sometimes pups will resist these exercises, others will appear unconcerned. In either case a caution is offered to those who plan to use them. Do not repeat them more than once per day and do not extend the time beyond that recommended for each exercise. Over stimulation of the neurological system can have adverse and detrimental results.

These exercises impact the neurological system by kicking it into action earlier than would be normally expected, the result being an increased capacity that later will help to make the difference in its performance. Those who play with their pups and routinely handle them should continue to do so because the neurological exercises are not substitutions for routine handling, play socialization or bonding.

Benefits of Stimulation

Five benefits have been observed in canines that were exposed to the Bio Sensor stimulation exercises. The benefits noted were:

1. Improved cardio vascular performance (heart rate)
2. Stronger heart beats,
3. Stronger adrenal glands,
4. More tolerance to stress, and
5. Greater resistance to disease.

In tests of learning, stimulated pups were found to be more active and were more exploratory than their non- stimulated littermates over which they were dominant in competitive situations.

Secondary effects were also noted regarding test performance. In simple problem solving tests using detours in a maze, the non-stimulated pups became extremely aroused, whined a great deal, and made many errors. Their stimulated littermates were less disturbed or upset by test conditions and when comparisons were made, the stimulated littermates were more calm in the test environment, made fewer errors and gave only an occasional distress sound when stressed.

Socialization

As each animal grows and develops, three kinds of stimulation have been identified that impact and influence how it will develop and be shaped as an individual. The first stage is called early neurological stimulation and the second stage is called socialization. The first two (early neurological stimulation and socialization) have in common a window of limited time. When Lorenz, (1935) first wrote about the importance of the stimulation process, he wrote about imprinting during early life and its influence on the later development of the individual. He states that it was different from conditioning in that it occurred early in life and took place very rapidly producing results which seemed to be permanent. One of the first and perhaps the most noted research effort involving the larger animals was achieved by Kellogg & Kellogg (1933). As a student of Dr. Kellogg's, I found him and his wife to have an uncanny interest in children and young animals and the changes and the differences that occurred during early development. Their history-making study involved raising their own newborn child with a newborn primate. Both infants were raised together as if they were twins.

This study, like others that followed attempted to demonstrate that among the mammals, there are great differences in their speed of physical and mental development. Some are born relatively mature and quickly capable of motion and locomotion, while others are very immature, immobile and slow to develop. For example, the Rhesus monkey shows rapid and precocious development at birth, while the chimpanzee and the other "great apes" take much longer. Last and slowest is the human infant.

One of the earliest efforts to investigate and look for the existence of socialization in canines was undertaken by Scott-

Fuller (1965). In their early studies, they were able to demonstrate that the basic technique for testing the existence of socialization was to show how readily adult animals would foster young animals, or accept one from another species. They observed that, with the higher level animals, it is easiest done by hand rearing. When the foster animal transfers its social relationships to the new species, researchers conclude that socialization has taken place. Most researchers agree that among all species, a lack of adequate socialization generally results in unacceptable behavior and often times produces undesirable aggression, excessiveness, fearfulness, sexual inadequacy and indifference toward partners.

Socialization studies confirm that one of the critical periods for humans (infant) to be stimulated are generally between three weeks and twelve months of age. For canines the period is shorter, between the fourth and sixteenth weeks of age. The lack of adequate social stimulation, such as handling, mothering and contact with others, adversely affects social and psychological development in both humans and animals. In humans, the absence of love and cuddling increases the risk of an aloof, distant, asocial or sociopathic individual. Over-mothering also has its detrimental effects by preventing sufficient exposure to other individuals and situations that have an important influence on growth and development. It occurs when a parent insulates the child from outside contacts or keeps the apron strings tight, thus limiting opportunities to explore and interact with the outside world. In the end, over-mothering generally produces a dependent, socially maladjusted and sometimes emotionally disturbed individual.

Protected youngsters who grow up in an insulated environment often become sickly, despondent, lacking in flexibility and unable to make simple social adjustments. Generally, they are unable to function productively or to interact successfully when they become adults.

Owners who have busy life styles with long and tiring work and social schedules often cause pets to be neglected. Left to themselves with only an occasional trip out of the house or off of the property they seldom see other canines or strangers and generally suffer from poor stimulation and socialization. For many, the side effects of loneliness and boredom set-in. The resulting behavior manifests itself in the form of chewing, digging, and hard- to-control behavior (Battaglia).

It seems clear that small amounts of stress followed by early socialization can produce beneficial results. The danger seems to be in not knowing where the thresholds are for over and under stimulation. Many improperly socialized youngsters develop into older individuals unprepared for adult life, unable to cope with its challenges, and interactions. Attempts to re-socialize them as adults have only produced small gains. These failures confirm the notion that the window of time open for early neurological and social stimulation only comes once. After it passes, little or nothing can be done to overcome the negative effects of too much or too little stimulation.

The third and final stage in the process of growth and development is called enrichment. Unlike the first two stages it has no time limit, and by comparison, covers a very long period of time. Enrichment is a term which has come to mean the positive sum of experiences which have a cumulative effect upon the individual. Enrichment experiences typically involve exposure to a wide variety of interesting, novel, and exciting experiences with regular opportunities to freely investigate, manipulate, and interact with them. When measured in later life, the results show that those reared in an enriched environment tend to be more inquisitive and are more able to perform difficult tasks.

The educational TV program called "Sesame Street" is perhaps the best known example of a children's enrichment program. The results show that when tested, children who regularly watched this program performed better than playmates who did not. Follow-up studies show that those who regularly watch "Sesame Street" tend to seek a college education and when enrolled, performed better than playmates who were not regular watchers of the "Sesame Street" program.

There are numerous children's studies that show the benefits of enrichment techniques and programs. Most focus on improving self-esteem and self-talk. Follow-up studies show that the enriched "Sesame Street" students, when later tested were brighter and scored above average, and most often were found to be the products of environments that contributed to their superior test scores. On the other hand, those whose test scores were generally below average, (labeled as dull) and the products of underprivileged or non- enriched environments, often had little or only small amounts of stimulation during early childhood and only minimal amounts of enrichment during their developmental and formative years. Many were characterized as children who grew up with little interaction with others, poor parenting, few toys, no books and a steady diet of TV soap operas.

A similar analogy can be found among canines. All the time they are growing they are learning because their nervous systems are developing and storing information that may be of inestimable use at a later date. Studies by Scott and Fuller confirm that non-enriched pups, when given free choice, preferred to stay in their kennels. Other littermates who were given only small amounts of outside stimulation between five and eight weeks of age were found to be very inquisitive and very active. When kennel doors were left open, the enriched pups would come bounding out while littermates who were not exposed to enrichment would remain behind. The non-stimulated pups would typically be fearful of unfamiliar objects and generally preferred to withdraw rather than investigate. Even well-bred pups of superior pedigrees would not explore or leave their kennels, and many were found difficult to train as adults. These pups, in many respects, were similar to the deprived children. They acted as if they had become institutionalized, preferring the routine and safe environment of their kennel to the stimulating world outside their immediate place of residence.

Regular trips to the park, shopping centers and obedience and agility classes serve as good examples of enrichment activities. Chasing and retrieving a ball on the surface seems to be enriching because it provides exercise and includes rewards. While repeated attempts to retrieve a ball provide much physical activity, it should not be confused with enrichment exercises. Such playful activities should be used for exercise and play or as a reward after returning from a trip or training session. Road work and chasing balls are not substitutes for trips to the shopping mall, outings or obedience classes most of which provide many opportunities for interaction and investigation.

Finally, it seems clear that stress early in life can produce beneficial results. The danger seems to be in not knowing where the thresholds are for over and under stimulation. The absence or the lack of adequate amounts of stimulation generally will produce negative and undesirable results. Based on the above, it is fair to say that the performance of most individuals can be improved, including the techniques described above. Each contributes in a cumulative way and supports the next stage of development.

Conclusion

Breeders can now take advantage of the information available to improve and enhance performance. Generally, genetics account for about 35% of the performance, but the remaining 65% (management, training, nutrition) can make the difference. In the management category, it has been shown that breeders should be guided by the rule that it is generally considered prudent to guard against under and over stimulation. Short of ignoring pups during their first two months of life, a conservative approach would be to expose them to children, people, toys and other animals on a regular basis. Handling and touching all parts of their anatomy is also a necessary part of their learning which can be started as early as the third day of life. Pups that are handled early and on a regular basis generally do not become hand-shy as adults.

Because of the risks involved in under-stimulation, a conservative approach to using the benefits of the three stages has been suggested based primarily on the works of Arskeusky, Kellogg, Yearkes and the "Bio Sensor" program (later known as the "Super Dog Program").

Both experience and research have dominated the beneficial effects that can be achieved via early neurological stimulation, socialization and enrichment experiences. Each has been used to improve performance and to explain the differences that occur between individuals, their trainability, health and potential. The cumulative effects of the three stages have been well documented. They best serve the interests of owners who seek high levels of performance when properly used. Each has a cumulative effect and contributes to the development and the potential for individual performance.

References:

1. Battaglia, C.L., "Loneliness and Boredom" Doberman Quarterly, 1982.

2. Kellogg, W.N. & Kellogg, The Ape and the Child, New York: McGraw Hill.

3. Scott & Fuller, (1965) Dog Behavior -The Genetic Basics, University Chicago Press.

4. Scott, J.P., Ross, S., A.E. and King D.K. (1959) The Effects of Early Enforced Weaning Behavior of Puppies, J. Genetics Psychologist, p 5: 261-81.

ABOUT THE AUTHOR

Carmen L Battaglia holds a Ph.D. and Masters Degree from Florida State University. As an AKC judge, researcher and writer, he has been a leader in promotion of breeding better dogs and has written many articles and several books.

Dr. Battaglia is also a popular TV and radio talk show speaker. His seminars on breeding dogs, selecting sires and choosing puppies have been well received by the breed clubs all over the country. Those interested in learning more about his seminars should contact him directly. Visit his website at http://www.breedingbetterdogs.com .

Early Stimulation Exercises

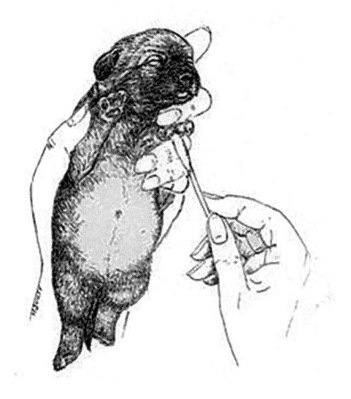

Figure # 1 Tactical stimulation

Figure # 2 Head held erect

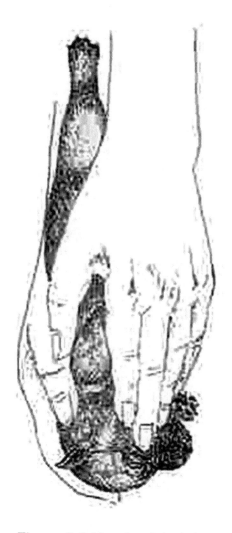

Figure # 3 Head pointed down

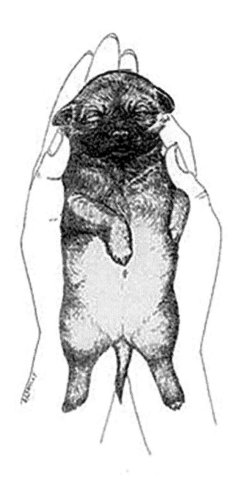

Figure # 4 Figure Supine position

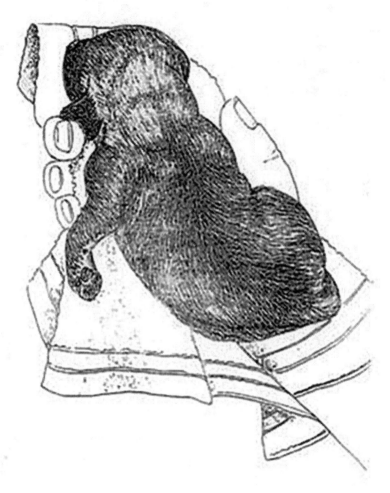

. Figure # 5 Thermal stimulation

Appendix 2

How One Breeder Sets Up Her Puppy Area

Laurel Cook and Ross McLaughlin of Culandubh Kennels in Ontario, Canada http://www.foxredlabs.ca supplied photos and the accompanying descriptions of her puppy area. I cannot thank them enough.

Our puppy raising setup provides this detour scenario. The pups can see through the wire when placed in the shavings area but have to detour through two openings in order to get to the other side of the wire (the tiled area) where food, playmates or people are located.

3.1.11 "If we want to challenge a pup physically to improve muscle coordination, we put up a barrier that he can see over but not through and can crawl over. To mentally challenge the pup in a detour problem, the barrier must be too high to crawl over or see over but one he can see through. The object the pup wants, such as food, a chew toy, another pup, is visible but attainable only if it goes around the barrier. A few detour problems will enable the pup to later solve a variety of problems, even those only vaguely related to the original detour problems. The dogs can solve other spatial problems that come up years later without need of a whole new learning regimen. They can also solve temporal problems such as how long is 10 minutes. No, it doesn't teach them how to tell time, but they learn patience, waiting for something they want is not much different from going away from something in order to get it, even going out of sight of it and approaching from a different angle. Mentally exercising pups gives them the capability to figure it out.

3.1.12 Self confidence in puppies can be increased by letting them learn how easy it is to go up a see through ramp and walk on an elevated see through bridge. It also improves perception of depth by challenging them with these visual cliffs. New experiences are most important. The more pups hear, smell, touch, chew on, investigate by all the means available, the better off they are for it. From 5 to 6 weeks onward, exposure to the world in the form of walks with littermates is easy experience to give them, weather conditions permitting. Every experience pups have will stimulate neural development and so brain development. As the brain develops, so does the learning ability, insight into problems and so problem solving ability, which in turn stimulates more neural development. The pup will then keep right on self-improving.

3.1.13 Therefore, besides the specifically related, distantly related, and even unrelated learning relationships, there is the overall general improvement in learning ability. A criterion of intelligence is elevated learning ability. By exercising the brain with mental challenges we improve the total brain function, not just one area of it. The breeder has the power to improve nerve conductivity in both speed and accuracy, recovery time of the neural synapses is shortened as the chemical and electrical signals react faster, and the nerves can fire repeatedly quicker. The brain mass increases dramatically as nerve cell density increases. Overall brain efficiency markedly improves. Just as the effect of physically challenging the muscular system, the whole body benefits, not just one part, so the whole brain and nervous system with all its neural and neurosecretory functions benefits from the challenges of mental exercise.

3.1.14 Most dogs are born with more mental capacity than we often understand. Whether the potential is realized, is in the hands of the breeder and in the environment set up for the pups. A sterile, coddling, do nothing environment produces sterile minded dogs. A challenging, stimulating environment that exercises both muscles and neurons produces pups that approach or even surpass their potential." quoted from an article in Retriever Journal

3.5 Physical obstacles, different surfaces, reactive toys. I have constructed several obstacles that I begin using in the puppy play area at about 3 ½ weeks of age. I begin with the "Castle" and then after a few days add in a ramp and then a few days latter a small teeter totter and then a few days later add a tunnel and so on. **Every day I rearrange the obstacles so that the pups face a slightly changed environment each day.** I have included some pictures of these.

3.5.1 The "Castle" - This is a baby play pen in which I have cut doors to allow the pups to start negotiating doors and a simple maze.

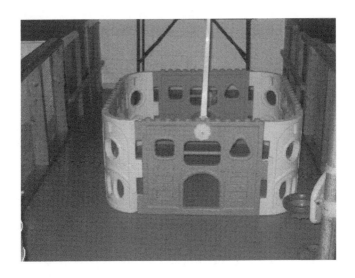

3.5.2 The Ramps - I have a smaller four sided ramp that I begin with. By the time the pups are older, I add a larger ramp.

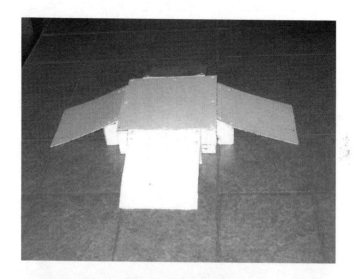

3.5.3 The Teeter Totters - I start with a small board with a 2 inch piece of PVC pipe as the fulcrum. By the time the pups are older, I use a teeter-totter with a 4 inch fulcrum.

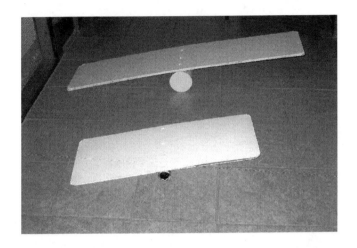

3.5.4 The Tires - I have a set of three wheel barrow tires that I have attached to boards for stabilization.

3.5.5 The Tunnels - I start with a 5 gallon pail with the bottom taken out and attached to a board to keep it stable. Then after a few days I place another similar bucket end to end with the first one and then a few days later I add a third one. Then after another week I will put out a child's play tunnel as well as a "Y" tunnel.

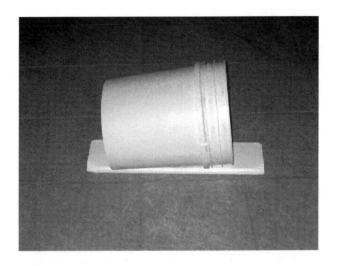

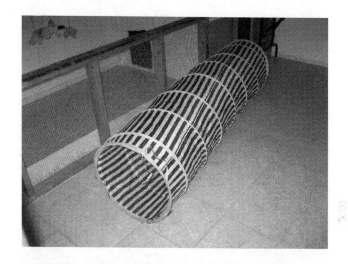

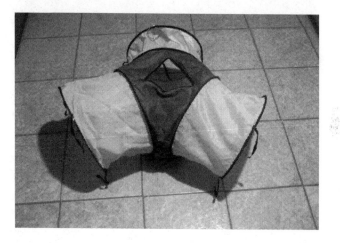

3.5.6 The Cookie Grates – I wired three baking cooling grates together to teach the pups to walk on grated surfaces.

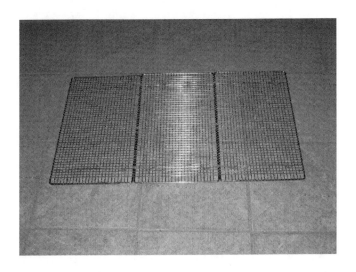

3.5.7 The Wobble Board – I use a square piece of plywood with a small box underneath that holds a ball. The board "wobbles" as the pups walk on it.

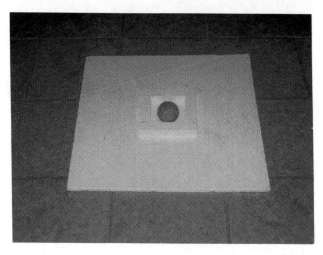

3.5.8 Reactive Toys – I use a baby mobile that turns and plays music to get the pups to look up for motion. I also have some baby toys that play tunes and flash lights when it is pushed.

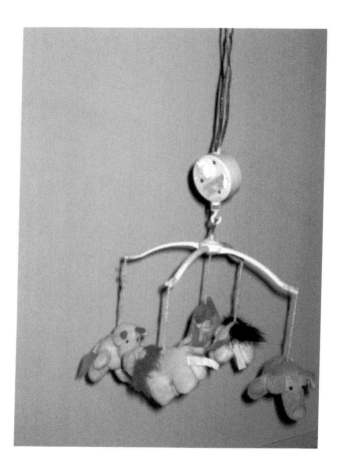

3.5.9 Combinations – Here are some pictures of the varied setup for obstacles:

I also constructed a modular "jungle gym" that can be rearranged in many ways to provide a different course each day for the puppies. I designed it so that it fits in the puppy area and the puppies must interact with the obstacles if they want to get from one end of the play area to the other. I start at 5 1/2 weeks of age and introduce a new part of the jungle gym each day so that by the time they are in their sixth week of age I can put together all of the obstacles into an integrated setup.

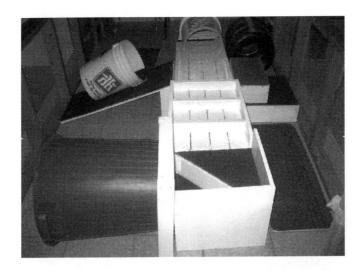

A mirror placed in the puppy area not only provides stimulation, but also helps improve visual acuity.

(If you would like to see the photos in color, these photos are in full color in the eBook http://tinyurl.com/no6udcw.)

Noise Phobia Prevention – Exposure to a wide range of sounds during puppyhood protects dogs from developing phobias as adults. Our puppies are born in our bedroom on the main floor of our house and spend the first three weeks there. One of the advantages of this is that the pups are exposed to the various noises of a busy household. At a Dr Ian Dunbar seminar several years ago, he pointed out that it is best to start exposing pups to loud noises as early as a few days old because their ears don't open until at least 7 – 10 days. Loud noises would be muffled when their ears are only partially opened and thus by the time their ears are fully opened, they have become accustomed to these louder noises without developing phobias. So I merrily bang pots around in the kitchen, vacuum around the puppy pen, play the DVD loudly and dance when nobody is watching. However, we found that some puppies still developed noise phobias for several sounds that were seasonal, intermittent or not heard within our household. Sounds such as thunderstorms or hot air balloons.

3.3 So I purchased a Sounds for Behaviour Therapy CD – A programme prepared at the UK Animal Behaviour Centre of Dr Roger Mugford. The CD has normal everyday sounds plus less frequently heard ones that are seasonal or intermittent such as fireworks, gunshots, hot air balloons, thunderstorms, etc. There are 30 sound tracks in total in 4 categories of sounds, each having several recordings with a playtime of approx 3 mins each;

a. Bangs

b. Transport

c. Household

d. People

3.4 For the first exposure, I play the CD at a barely audible level when puppies are comfortable, such as at nursing time or when they are distracted with play. Gradually over the course of two to three weeks I increase the volume by small increments. Remember to start the CD at different tracks each time. The first time I used the CD, I put it on when the puppies were nursing and by the time they hit the thunderstorm track, they were falling asleep. I kept starting the CD at the beginning each day but the pups did not stay awake long enough to get past the thunderstorm track very often.

Then a few weeks later, I had some children in the puppy pen playing with the pups and I thought it would be a great opportunity to get through the entire CD as the children would keep them awake for some time. However, when the thunderstorm track started to play, all of the pups immediately stopped playing, ran into their bed and went to sleep! A year later, I asked one of the owners of a pup from that litter how her dog behaved during a thunderstorm. She happily told me that her dog had no problem with thunderstorms, whenever one started, the dog simply came and curled up on her feet and went to sleep…Although I thought I was preventing noise phobias, in fact I was only preventing noise phobias for the noises on the CD before thunderstorms and conditioning them to go to sleep during thunderstorms. Lesson learned….

Appendix 3

What is Puppy License?

All of a sudden when your puppy is about five months old, older dogs – both your older dog and other people's older dogs – all of whom used to love your sweet puppy seem to attack him for no reason. You become alarmed and think there is something wrong with the other dog and it should be disciplined. Generally, that's not the case. What has happened is that your puppy has outgrown its puppy license.

What Puppy License Is, When It Happens, Why It Happens

Puppy license is when puppies do whatever they want to an older dog whenever they want to do it without any inhibition usually with no repercussions. Up until about five months, there are seldom corrections or punishment for unruly, rude, pushy, demanding behavior UNTIL...

Puppies, like children, can engage in behaviors that older dogs and people would never accept in adult dogs or older children. For example, if your toddler is standing next to you and grabs your pants leg to get your attention, that is normal behavior. But that exact same behavior is not acceptable from a teenager. A similar thing happens with dogs. Normal behaviorally healthy adult dogs will tolerate behaviors (listed below) from puppies that they would never tolerate from other adult dogs.

As your puppy develops, his mother and littermates teach him rules on how to behave – "I'm trying to get some sleep. Leave me alone NOW" from mom. She raises her lip, growls, and then snaps at the puppy. He learns what mom's body language means. Or from a sibling, "You just bit me too hard; I'm not going to play with you," so he learns bite inhibition.

Up until the puppy license expires, any corrections or punishment are usually pretty benign. But now he is an adolescent and on his way to becoming an adult, so the physicality of the corrections increases. He has one foot in the puppy world and one foot in the adult world. His brain may still be a puppy brain, but his body is becoming an adult's body. His status has changed, and the simple puppy corrections he was given don't seem to cut it anymore. He's just not getting the message by asking, so now he has to be TOLD in no uncertain terms. It's the equivalent of our shouting.

Puppies think the world revolves around them and that they are the kings of the universe – until they outgrow a boundary that they did not know existed and someone teaches them the rules, which is at about five months. Everything changes because the adult hormones kick in and the smell of puppy urine changes. Your puppy now is an adolescent, with all the behavior issues of adolescence – testing boundaries, forgetting every rule they once knew, questioning authority, and being an all-around jerk.

This seems to be more pronounced in males because this time is when the testosterone kicks in. To make things worse, testosterone levels increase until the puppy is about ten months old at which time he has five times the testosterone in his system – yikes! – as he will when he is a fully matured adult unless, of course, he is neutered.   Even if he is neutered, he still goes through these behavioral changes although they do not seem to be as pronounced.   But his behavior still needs to be corrected so he can integrate into adult dog society.

The period when puppy license expires is crucial for puppies because they learn what is and is not acceptable behavior around other dogs. If he does not learn this – if we interrupt the lessons – then he will not be a behaviorally healthy adult.

The Lesson

At their core, behaviorally fit dogs do not want to hurt or kill other dogs – it just ain't a good idea for perpetuating the species! So they have developed ritualized behaviors and escalations of warning signals so they do not have to resort to fighting. Each lesson has a beginning, a middle, and an end. If we interrupt, then the puppy never learns the end and the adult dog may have to intensify the next encounter to make sure that the puppy understands, and THAT encounter may lead to bloodshed.

- The beginning is the puppy performing the behavior.
- The middle is the adult dog correcting him.
- The end is the puppy saying "I'm sorry" and the adult saying, "It's not you I don't like; it's *your behavior* I don't like."

Puppy Behavior

Here are some behaviors that may have been previously tolerated by other dogs but now are not. The puppy:

- Barks, demanding that the older dog give him the toy
- Barks, demanding to play
- Barks in the older dog's face
- Barks for attention
- Barks just because.......
- Challenges the older dog
- Claims the older dog's bed as his own
- Jumps on the older dog
- Lies in wait and pounces on the older dog
- Mounts the older dog either from the back, on the side, or on its head
- Muzzle punches the older dog
- Paws at the older dog
- Steals food or toys from the older dog

Normal Older Dog Response

The older dog warns the puppy and generally follows a pattern in this order (which may vary a bit depending on the breed):

- Freezes
- Stares at the puppy
- Lifts his lip
- Growls
- Barks
- Snaps
- Muzzle grabs the puppy and/or
- Pins the puppy or knocks him down
- Stands over the puppy

All of this may happen so quickly that if we blink, then we miss it! But the puppy gets the message.

Or the response may be longer with a scuffle occurring and the puppy screaming – not because he's being hurt but because this REALLY is a shock to him. It may even look like the dogs are fighting, but a behaviorally sound older dog does not harm the puppy.

The Puppy's Normal Response

This is how the puppy says "I'm sorry":

- Arching his back
- Crawling or lowering his body
- Holding his head downwards
- Holding his tail down with a minimal wag or tucked between his rear legs
- Leaving the area
- Licking the lips of the older dog
- Lifting a front paw
- Looking away
- Pulling his ears back and pinning them to the side of his head
- Rolling on his back
- Screaming as if he is being maimed
- Slinking away
- Urinating

What Is Not Normal

- If the encounter results in wounds with blood and it requires veterinary treatment. Someone has gone too far and you need to get help immediately.
- If your puppy does not submit to the older dog, get a behavior consultant in fast.
- If the older dog follows the puppy by moving slowly toward your puppy as a target
- If the older dog stares intently at your puppy with his ears forward
- If the older dog bullies your puppy.
  - o Chases your puppy so he cannot get away
  - o Stalks or lies in wait to trounce on your puppy
  - o Moves towards your puppy with his tail high and stiff
  - o Has piloerection – the hair on his back standing on end
- If your puppy is extremely fearful of that specific dog
- If the older dog picks up your puppy by the scruff of the neck and shakes him. If you see this, intervene *immediately* because this is a kill bite.

If the older dog has not met your puppy, then he may not be so forgiving. I have heard more than once, "I asked the owner if their dog was friendly, and they said yes. So I let them play. And then their dog bit my puppy." Be VERY careful about which dogs you let play with your puppy because:

- The owner may be clueless about dog behavior.
- The dog may never have learned proper dog communication skills.
- The dog may be ill or have something physically wrong.

- The dog may be shy, and the interaction with an unknown exuberant puppy is too much for him.
- Your puppy is not part of the dog's family, and he feels no need to treat his indiscretions civilly.
- The dog may not allow the puppy to move away.
- The dog may not acknowledge your puppy's appeasement signals and continues or escalates the correction.
- The dog may interpret your puppy's crying as the screams of prey. Predation is controlled by a different part of the brain; and once it is triggered, it is difficult to stop until the prey is killed.

What People Should Do

LEAVE THE DOGS ALONE for the most part – except if the older dog displays one of the abnormal behaviors listed above – and let the older dog correct the puppy. This is difficult for most people – it's similar to taking your child to the doctor to get a vaccine. You know he is going to cry because it hurts, but the shot will protect him from some terrible diseases. It's hard to watch as he gets hurt, but the effects will last a lifetime.

If you think you can "teach him the lesson," you can't! Why?:

- Your timing is nowhere as accurate as a dog's timing.
- You may interfere at the wrong instant so the lesson is not learned – or a completely different lesson is taught.
- The older dog is teaching the puppy a lesson that needs to be played out to its conclusion in a language your puppy understands.

- Your puppy may think that you will always "rescue" him and either will form an alliance with you against your older dog or will never develop the confidence he needs.
- Your older dog will not understand your interference.

Here are some Additional Do's and Don'ts:

- Don't try to do a muzzle grab yourself because
  o You can get bitten.
  o You are not quick enough.
  o Your puppy may learn that your hands near his face mean pain, so he will bite you first and ask questions later. Since you are the role model, that will translate to your dog that other people's hands near his face equal bad stuff – not what you want if someone innocently tries to pet him or if your vet is trying to examine him.
- Don't force the dogs to interact – let it flow naturally.
- Try to make sure that the dogs can get away from each other in the future.
- Don't leave food or toys around to "see if the puppy has learned his lesson or how it's going to play out."
- Don't comfort the puppy even if you may be tempted. Part of the lesson is that the puppy has to learn no one is going to reward him for the dumb thing that he did.
- Do make sure they are not confined together until there is a firm pecking order established.
- Do supervise their interactions for several days or even weeks until they re-establish their ranking order.
- Do GET HELP sooner rather than later. If you wait, then not only is someone going to be injured, but you are going to have veterinary and/or doctor bills AND have to

pay for a behavior consultant or have to rehome one of the dogs.

◆◆◆◆◆◆◆◆◆◆◆◆◆◆

I was lucky to find **Adrienne Farricelli** who kindly allowed me to include her article which gives another terrific explanation of puppy license.

What is a puppy License? And What is its Purpose?

Among the interactions taking place in a social group of dogs, many different and interesting behaviors may be observed. Normally, when puppies are born, right after weaning, they are granted what is known as a "puppy license". What exactly is a puppy license and what does it entail?

Generally, when the puppies are very small, they interact primarily with their mothers. About 90% of the time is spent sleeping while the rest is spent nursing and being cleaned by the mother. Mother dog is protective during this stage as the puppies are very vulnerable. Once the puppies' eyes open, they may start crawling around and exploring the world around them. As the puppies moves about, they start interacting with other dogs in their social group.

Normal social dogs know for a fact that the puppy is small and tends to behave in a "socially illiterate" manner. While the mother dog and litter mates have taught some social rules such as bite inhibition and submissive postures, there is still a lot to learn. A good part of learning good canine etiquette comes from the exposure to healthy, well-socialized adult dogs which are part of the social group. The role of these dogs is to guide the puppy and teach the youngster which behaviors are appropriate and which are not.

Puppies also often engage in behaviors that make clear they are just puppies and as such, should have a puppy license. When an older dog approaches, the puppy may engage in appeasement behaviors which are telling the older dog **"I am just a small puppy, please don't hurt me"**. Whining, submissive postures such as ears, back, licking the lips of the older dog and keeping the head and body low are all non-threatening signals. When the puppy rolls over his back and emits a dribble of urine, this urine further proves his right to this license. **Indeed, the urine of a puppy advertises the puppy's age as well.**

It is as if the puppy was saying **"See? Even my urine smell tells you I am just a puppy! I don't know any better and I really did not mean to bite your ears and tail but they look like so much fun to play!"** The older dogs understand this and tend to close an eye. They are more likely to accept these behaviors compared to how they would react if this was an adult dog. Things, however, start to change as the puppy matures, which brings to the next question; when does a puppy license expire?

When Does a Puppy License Expire?

As the puppy matures, the urine components tend to change. Testosterone levels tend to rise in the urine when the puppy reaches five months old. The biggest surge, takes place when the puppy is 10 months old, with levels reaching up to seven times more actual normal levels found in adult dogs. Then, once the puppy is about 18 months, these levels revert to the normal levels found in adult dogs.

Upon detecting these hormonal levels, older dogs revoke the puppy license and think about putting the testing youngster into his place before he becomes a significant challenge. This is when the puppy license privileges abruptly stop.

But My Older Dogs will not Grant a Puppy License!

Yet, if a puppy license does exist, why are there so many people having trouble with older dogs not being willing to accept puppies? One great answer comes from Mario Sturm author of the book *100 Mistakes in Dog Training: The Somewhat Practical Guide to Buying a Puppy, Training and Dealing With Dogs.*

The Puppy is Not Part of The Pack!

While it is true that puppy licenses do exist, it is important to keep in mind that these mainly apply to puppies that are part of a social group of wolves or free-ranging dogs, basically a family. Note: to learn more on these social structures read David Mech's studies on social structures in wolves.

Things may change drastically when an unknown puppy that is not related to any other member is introduced to a group of dogs. **An unfamiliar puppy is of course not part of the social group, and therefore, will not typically be granted such a license.** This means you should practice caution and never assume nothing will ever happen to your puppy because of the "puppy license warranty".

This also means that there may be chances your older dog may be a bit more lenient with the puppy, but to err on the side of caution, **you should also expect your older dog may not be willing to accept misbehavior as expected, which may lead to squabbles.**

The Puppy May Appear Threatening

Adult dogs who have never been exposed to puppies before may be stressed by the rowdy puppy behaviors. Some adult dogs barely tolerate other dogs and a puppy may be too much for them. They may try to avoid the puppy or attack the puppy if the puppy does not take the warning signs of stress and growing intolerance seriously. Some dog owners, especially those owning an elderly dog, find that their dog does better when the puppy is calmer. **For this reason, it helps to keep the two separated at first and then present the puppy when it is tired and less likely to engage in excessively rowdy behaviors.**

It is at times a big mistake to adopt a puppy to "rejuvenate" a dog that is getting old. The old dog may have a hard time telling the puppy to stop and with the pain of arthritis or other medical issues, the older dog may not be much in the mood for play. **A puppy should not be constantly pestering an older dog that just wants to relax and conduct a laid-back life.**

Puppy License Does not Mean Permissiveness

Another important clarification to keep in mind is that a puppy license does not translate into an adult dog **accepting anything** the puppy does. Adult dogs are there to teach the puppy proper behaviors and they may resort to discipline to put the puppy into place. A certain amount of discipline must be dished out by the adult dog to train good dog etiquette. This often entails physical punishment. In such cases, the physical punishment is more a form of ritualized aggression than anything else. In other words, no real harm is done to the puppy.

This form of discipline tells the puppy when to back off, how to ask permission, how to submit and which behaviors are appropriate and not. **Because it may be challenging at**

times to tell if the dog is really engaging in harmless discipline or if there is something more serious going on, the intervention of a behavior specialist may be required. The reasons for the intervention are several. A behavior specialist would be able to tell:

- If the adult dog is engaging in discipline or if there is more into it
- If the puppy is able to send appeasement signals to the adult dog
- If the adult dog is capable of reading these appeasement signals
- If the puppy is actually learning from the adult dog and how it responds
- If the puppy appears traumatized by the discipline or if it does not affect the puppy at all
- If the interaction should be stopped or allowed to continue
- If the puppy and adult dog should not be allowed to interact any more with the option of re-homing one of the two or keeping them permanently separated.

The latter is very important. If the adult dog is truly engaging in discipline, it is important to allow for him to finish giving the "lecture". **If the adult dog is interrupted, the puppy may never learn appropriate and inappropriate behaviors and the adult dog may feel the need to escalate into more effective strategies, which may ultimately harm the puppy.**

Note: Never allow an adult dog to pick up a puppy and shake the puppy as he does with a toy. That is dangerous and can even kill the puppy! Also, be on the look out for an adult dog that does not accept appeasement signals and that does not allow the puppy to leave the room or escape.

Generally, in cases where the adult dog disciplines the puppy without doing any visible harm, the interactions do not require intervention no matter how noisy and dramatic. Puppies upon being corrected may emit a high-pitched yelp as if hurt, but this is mostly drama as the adult dog most likely did not even make contact. Keep in mind that if **the adult really wanted to hurt the puppy he would.** After the discipline takes place, the puppy may show submissive gestures such as licking the mouth or moving away with its body low. **The puppy most likely learns the lesson and the adult dog may continue teaching the puppy, perhaps next time warning with just a mere stare or a light growl.** Do not feel tempted to comfort the puppy or punish the adult in such a case.

Important considerations: always supervise the adult and puppy interactions. Do not leave food or toys around as these may cause tension. Make sure your puppy has an escape route so to move away from the interaction as needed. Intervene if the behavior is more than just ritualized discipline and consult with a certified applied animal behaviorist at once if something concerns you.

Disclaimer: this article is not to be used as a substitute for a hands-on behavioral assessment. If your adult dog shows worrisome behaviors towards your puppy, intervene immediately to stop the interaction, keep both parties separated and consult with a certified applied animal behaviorist.

Alexadry © Adrienne Farricelli, All Rights Reserved,

Adrienne Farricelli is Certified Professional Dog Trainer (CPDT-KA) and dog behavior consultant. She is owner and trainer of Rover's Ranch Home Cageless Boarding and Training, based in Huachuca City, Arizona. http://www.roversranchhome.com Her articles about dogs appear on several websites, print magazines and newsletters. Her personal blog is at: http://alexadry.hubpages.com/

Appendix 4

Normal and Abnormal
Puppy Behavior and Health,

Including Common Owner Complaints

Normal Puppy Behavior

- Acting alert and animated
- Acting bold and curious
- Acting cautious but curious
- Adapting to changes
- Affectionate
- Avoiding extended eye contact
- Barking
- Being able to be left alone for reasonable periods of time without whining or barking
- Being able to settle and relax
- Being active and energetic
- Being easily distracted
- Biting at and gnawing your hands, arms, and feet
- Biting at clothing and hair
- Chasing anything that moves

- Enjoying being around adults and children of all ages
- Enjoying being around dogs and puppies
- Enjoying human contact, being touched all over his body, and tolerating restraint
- Exhibiting the "puppy crazies" where he runs around like his tail is on fire
- Following someone everywhere
- Friendly to people and dogs
- Having a short attention span
- Jumping up on people and children and knocking them over
- Jumping up or trying to jump onto furniture and beds
- Mouthing or chewing everything – table legs, carpets, curtains, plants, CDs, books, personal belongings, clothing
- Pawing, batting at, or pouncing on toys or people
- Playing tug-o-war with plants, clothes, or his leash
- Playing well with dogs and cats
- Playing with your children's toys and/or destroying them
- Pulling cushions and pillows off the sofa to play with and/or shredding them
- Pulling items out of cabinets, closets, laundry baskets, and trash cans
- Putting everything he can find into his mouth
- Recovering quickly from being startled or frightened
- Relinquish control of food, toys, and other objects
- Rolling in smelly things
- Rolling over on his back
- Shaking toys vigorously
- Shredding his bed, soft toys, children's toys

- Shredding paper and taking tissues from wastebaskets
- Sleeping frequently and at odd times
- Sniffing and investigating everything
- Twitching during sleep
- Urinating frequently including every time he drinks, sleeps, wakes up, plays or goes out
- Vocalizing (growling and/or barking) during play
- Wanting to be near you
- Wanting to interact with you
- Wanting to play with everything
- Wanting to touch you while he's sleeping
- Whining, crying, or whimpering for short periods of time

Abnormal or Problematic Behavior

- Acting clingy, afraid to let owner out of sight
- Attacking other people or other pets in a threatening manner
- Avoiding being touched
- Avoiding children
- Avoiding interacting
- Backing away, ducking from touch, or acting fearful
- Barking back at you when being reprimanded
- Barking or crying constantly
- Being needy constantly
- Biting hard or attempting hard bites towards people or animals
- Circling continuously
- Crying constantly

- Cowering and cringing
- Disinterest in people and dogs
- Disliking being held or touched
- Fearing new situations
- Fighting an adult dog when he's being disciplined
- Freezing and stopping chewing as someone approaches and then beginning to chew after the person has gone past him – blocking the food with his body, eating faster, or raising his tail stiffly
- Growling and/or showing his teeth to make something or someone go away
- Growling if you try to take something from his mouth
- Growling or snarling except during play
- Guarding toys or food
- Hiding in corners or under furniture
- Inability to concentrate or focus attention for brief periods
- Lacking interest in children, adults, or other animals
- Leaning against you around children, adults, or animals
- Lunging and barking at people or dogs
- Moving away from people
- Quivering or shivering frequently
- Repetitive behavior
- Repetitive whining
- Resistance to grooming
- Shaking you off after you've touched him
- Showing the whites of his eye
- Staring at nothing
- Staring hard at people or animals
- Stiffening or growling when petted

- Taking toys or bones in another room, under a piece of furniture, or in his crate
- Tolerating but not enjoying non-family members, especially children
- Whining constantly

Please note: What is normal behavior for one breed and the degree that the puppy engages in that behavior may be more pronounced than for another breed. For example, labs are *very* mouthy – they were bred to use their mouths and retrieve game. So a lab puppy is going to be mouthier than a Maltese. And it's also going to be more pronounced *to you* since the lab is bigger than the Maltese. The lab's bite hurts more since his teeth are bigger and there is more force behind his bite because of his size.

Another thing to consider is that breed traits are more apparent. Beagles, which are scent hounds, sniff the ground a LOT and are interested in smells. Herding dogs are more interested in movement. That, however, does not mean that beagles will not run after things that move or that herders will not sniff the ground. But the proportion of the dog's time spent with the function he was bred for will be more pronounced. And some breeds are more socially oriented than others. A Cavalier King Charles, which was bred as a companion dog, is going to be more people oriented than a Jack Russell, which was bred to kill vermin.

As your puppy gets older, he will be less dependent on you and more interested in the environment, and his breed characteristics will begin to show themselves. His behavior will change dramatically from one week to the next, sometimes from one day to the next. It's not uncommon for the sweetest puppies to change into little demons in a week!

Common Puppy Owner Complaints

Please note that common puppy "problems" are normal puppy behavior!!!

- Attention seeking
- Barking, crying, whining
- Begging, stealing, scavenging food, clothing, other objects
- Chewing
- Digging
- Getting on furniture
- Housetraining accidents
- Hyperactivity
- Jumping up
- Jumping out of reach
- Mouthing
- Mounting
- Nipping
- Not coming when called
- Playing roughly
- Pulling on leash
- Running away
- Stealing
- Submissive urination

Normal Health

- Abdomen – firm but not hard, slightly rounded
- Appetite – good, likes food and likes to eat
- Belly – firm
- Breath – clean, fresh
- Coat/skin – soft, shining, clean smelling , smooth, elastic
- Ears – clean, pink, odor free
- Eyes – bright, clear, clean
- Foot pads – firm clean
- Gait – moves easily, no limping
- Genitals – clean, pink
- Gums – pink , firm
- Legs – straight (unless breed standard is different)
- Mouth – clean, no bad odor
- Muscles – flexible
- Nose – wet, not running, slightly damp, clean, cool
- Rectum – clean, pink, no blood or diarrhea
- Rib cage – firm, barrel-like
- Skin – pink, clean, odorless, firm and elastic but not tight, supple, smooth
- Spine – straight, even
- Stool – firm
- Teeth – white
- Weight – can feel ribs but ribs are not protruding

Abnormal Health

- Abdomen – distended, hard to the touch or flabby and wrinkled, sensitive
- Appetite – eating feces, disinterest in food
- Coat/skin – crusting, scaling, fleas and ticks, inflammations, oiliness, bald spots, dandruff, sores, redness, discolored areas, lumps, red spots, odorous, lack of elasticity, dry
- Coughing frequently
- Ears – matter in ears, bad odor, dirty or caked earflap, sensitive to touch, scratching, not reacting to noises
- Eyes – difficulty focusing
- Eyes – runny, cloudy, discharge, watering, squinting in light
- Foot pads – sore, cut or torn, ragged nails
- Genitals – pus or yellow discharge around sheath/vulva, undescended testicles
- Heavy water intake
- Lethargy or tiring easily
- Licking and/or chewing constantly
- Mouth – bad odor, bleeding gums, coated tongue, drooling, sensitive, discolored
- Nose – runny, discharge matter, hot
- Rectum – discharge, crusting, or dried feces, red
- Rib cage – frail, sore to touch
- Sneezing frequently
- Spine – bumps, knobs, sore to touch
- Tilting or shaking the head
- Twitching

- Vomiting
- Wheezing

Appendix 5

Hand Shyness

The idea behind this exercise is for your puppy to gradually get used to people's hands near his head. Begin training with the person who your puppy is MOST comfortable with, which is probably you.

It is important that he not get stressed during any of these sessions. If he starts exhibiting any signs of stress or snaps at you or becomes uncomfortable, then you have gone too far too fast. Go back to the previous step when he was okay and repeat that step several more times before proceeding to the next step.

Do the steps and sessions in order, and please do not skip any. Try to do several short sessions per day – no more than about a minute each. They go very quickly.

The person who your puppy is most comfortable with should complete the entire exercise to its conclusion. Then the next most comfortable does the exercises. Then the next most comfortable, etc.

Objective: to get your puppy used to hands around his face.

Position: You are facing each other.

Treat: in your right hand if you are right handed and vice-versa. Your right hand is your "treat-hand." Your left hand is your "empty-hand."

FIRST SESSION

- Begin feeding your puppy treats from your treat-hand one at a time. Put the treats right in front of his mouth so all he has to do is open his mouth and you can pop the treat in. He does not have to follow any command to get the treat.

- After the third treat, bring your empty-hand up to the side of his face about three inches away. Don't touch him, but just have that hand there immediately after delivering the treat, and then immediately take it away.

- Repeat the sequence at least ten times – treat from right treat-hand first, then left empty-hand at the side of his face – treat-hand/empty-hand – treat-hand/empty-hand – treat-hand/empty-hand, etc.

SECOND SESSION

Review the exercise by doing treat-hand/empty-hand three times.

He's used to the order of treat-hand/empty-hand, so now you're going to reverse the order.

Put your empty left hand next to his face and then immediately feed him a treat from your right treat-hand. He may startle at first, so that's why you need to give him the treat immediately. Now the order is empty-hand/treat-hand – empty-hand/treat-hand – empty-hand/treat-hand, etc. Repeat this several times. He should become comfortable with your switching the order after the first couple times. If he does not, then repeat the First Session as many times as necessary.

SUBSEQUENT SESSIONS

Rather than repeating the directions for each session, I'm just summing up what each session should consist of. **Each numbered entry is an entire session, and the format for each session is the same:**

- Begin each session with a review of the last session beginning with treat-hand/empty-hand.
- After the third treat, bring your empty-hand to the desired position.
- Repeat the treat-hand/empty-hand sequence at least ten times or until he is comfortable.
- Then switch to empty-hand/treat-hand.
- Be sure he is comfortable at the current step before proceeding to the next step.

  (In a nutshell, the sequence is treat-hand/empty-hand – treat-hand/empty-hand – treat-hand/empty-hand, etc. Then empty-hand/treat-hand – empty-hand/treat-hand – empty-hand/treat-hand, etc.)

These are the subsequent sessions:

1. Touch the side of his head with your empty-hand.
2. Put your empty-hand near the base of his ear.
3. Touch the base of his ear.

4. Put your empty-hand near the top of his head.
5. Touch the top of his head.
6. Put your empty-hand at the top of his head and pet him.
7. Put your empty-hand at the top of his head and pet him a bit harder – this simulates how other people will pet your puppy.

NEXT

- Repeat the entire sequence in several locations inside your house.
- Repeat the entire sequence in several locations outside your house.
- Repeat the entire sequence from the beginning with the person your puppy is next most comfortable with.
- Repeat the sequence with other family members or persons whom your puppy likes. When a nonfamily member is working with your dog, let your puppy see that you are giving control of him to the other person, i.e., let him see you hand the leash to that person.
- Repeat the sequence with persons whom your dog has met but has not interacted with.

Unfortunately, there will be a time when a stranger is going to pet your puppy/dog without asking permission. The purpose of this exercise is to prepare your puppy so he can get used to other people petting him so he will not be afraid or try to bite them.

Appendix 6

About Stress and Fear

How Can I Tell if My Puppy is Stressed?

Sometimes despite your best efforts, your puppy may become stressed. All stress is not bad! Stress is actually a good thing; too much stress is not. Don't pamper your puppy and do everything for him so he is never stressed. If you do, then when he is an adult, he has not learned coping skills and has two options in the way he shows stress – to be fearful and fall apart or to be aggressive and lash out.

Dogs show signs of stress before they go into a fearful state, so look for the signs and end the session before he gets fearful. If you see any of the stress signs, then don't panic! Your puppy needs you to be calm, so have a plan.

If he is afraid, try to reduce the strength of the source of the stress. Sometimes it's easy to determine the source – your puppy tries to run away from a vacuum cleaner. Sometimes it's not so obvious – your puppy feels uncomfortable around your neighborhood, but you don't know why.

What should his body look like? Loosey goosey. Relaxed. Wanting to engage. Or maybe ignoring. He does not necessarily have to be wagging his tail ferociously. But here's the stress signals to look for:

- Body or demeanor
  - Attention seeking
  - Breathing changes – either faster or slower
  - Crouching
  - Exposing his tummy
  - Freezing in place
  - Hyperactivity
  - Leaning or climbing on you
  - Lowering his body
  - Mounting
  - Moving slowly
  - Moving stiffly
  - Nervousness
  - Over reacting
  - Pace change (slowing down, speeding up, zigzagging, bolting)
  - Quiet and withdrawn
  - Restlessness
  - Scratching the invisible flea
  - Shaking as if he were wet
  - Stretching
  - Sweating from the pads of his feet
  - Trembling
  - Trying to move away, hide, or escape
  - Urinating or defecating
- Face or head
  - Head turned to the side
  - Lowering his head
  - Panting even though it is not hot
  - Wrinkled forehead

- Eyes
  - o Averting his eyes by looking away
  - o Blinking quickly
  - o Dilated pupils
  - o Drooling
  - o Looking quickly
  - o Staring intensely
- Ears
  - o Flattening his ears against his head
  - o Lowering his ears
  - o Moving his ears
- Mouth
  - o Closing his mouth when it was open and relaxed
  - o Corner of his mouth back
  - o Licking body parts
  - o Licking his nose
  - o Teeth chattering
  - o Tongue flicking
  - o Tongue withdrawn
  - o Yawning
- Tail
  - o Lowering his tail – the lower it is, the more stressed
- Vocalizing
  - o Barking, especially high pitched
  - o Whining

Something else to look for is even though he does not move, he may be shutting down. Don't mistake the absence of movement as proof that he is okay. Look at his whole body. Do an Internet search on dog body language so you can see how his body reflects what's going on in his mind.

Additionally, you can also find some excellent books here http://www.dogbookslibrary.com/dog-body-language.php

If you see the signals, do one or more of the procedures below:

- Act silly and upbeat
- Direct people how to approach your puppy
- Distract your puppy with something else such as throwing a ball
- Have an escape route
- Have him do an obedience exercise such as Sit (not Down)
- Introduce something he likes such as giving him a delicious treat
- Leave the location completely
- Lower the volume of a sound
- Move quickly past the scary thing (but not frantically!)
- Move to a place that is more distant from the scary thing
- Position yourself between your puppy and the scary thing
- Retreat and come toward it in baby steps and rewarding each baby step
- Sing songs especially nursery rhymes
- Target (see Targeting in Appendix 7 for directions)

And remember what the stressor was by remembering as much as the environment as you can.

- How close was the scary thing
- What were the sounds and smells
- Who was there

- What was the location or environment (in the bathroom or on the street, in your garage or in the driveway?)

Rather than forcing him into accepting the scary thing, you should slow down. You need to gauge his fear. Does he go towards it, retreat, and come back cautiously? Good. Then reward each step forward. Don't lure him toward the scary thing, but reward each step that he takes voluntarily. Sometimes you can just have a trail of treats towards the scary thing that he can eat and self reward. Then give him a jackpot when he finally reaches it. Be careful in your exuberance – sometimes you can get overzealous – "YIPPEE!!!" – when all you needed was a simple "good dog." If your reaction is over the top, that can frighten him yet again.

If these procedures are not working for you or if your puppy has fear of everything, the best thing you can do for you and your dog is to find a qualified trainer or behavior consultant who knows how to help. How do you choose the right one? Ask a hypothetical question – let's say your dog is afraid of slippery or shiny floors. Ask how that trainer/consultant would help. If the answer is to put him on a leash and drag him across the floor, find someone else.

What is a fear period?

Dogs can be fearful of something specific at any time in their lives. However, there are predictable fear periods as they are developing when it seems like they are afraid of everything, even if that same thing was okay yesterday. During all these fear periods, try to keep your puppy from having any traumatic experiences, especially during the first fear period.

- The first period begins when he is approximately five weeks old (which is the one we are concerned with in this book), escalates at the end of the seventh week, and lasts about three weeks.

- The second is around six months during adolescence, and the larger the dog, the longer it can last, up to about 14 months.

- And finally there may be a third in early adulthood, which is anywhere from ten months on; again, the larger the dog, the later it will be.

How does your puppy look? Is his tail between his legs? Is he trying to run away? Is he trying to bite you? Are his ears back? Is he breathing heavily? Then he is frightened. If he is frightened and you pick him up and tell him everything is okay, you think you are soothing him. But that may not be the case.

There was a time not too long ago that trainers would tell you not to tell him everything is okay because you were rewarding the fear. Dog training is a fairly new profession and is evolving, so our beliefs are evolving as we learn more. Fear is an emotion, and an emotion just is. It cannot be rewarded. What you see is what you get. However, as you try to soothe him, because *you* may sound whiny or talk to him in a high-pitched voice as well as having a concerned look on your face, he interprets those actions as *your* being afraid – and that's not what you want to do.

Comforting him is okay as long as you are not whining – "Oh, what a silly dog" said in a matter-of-fact voice and with a smile on your face versus a concerned look and a high-pitched "Oh, snookums, is that mean thing scaring you? Mommy will take care of you."

So, act upbeat, talk to him in a positive voice, try to play a game. If he is still frightened, then take him some distance from the scary thing and then act silly, etc. Do some Sits – don't do Downs because that's probably too overwhelming for him. Teach him to target. (See Targeting in Appendix 7.) Your role in this is to show him there is nothing to be afraid of and that you will take care of him and protect him. Don't overwhelm him by going too far too fast because you will only make the situation worse.

What not to do

- Don't punish fearful behavior.
- Don't force him to interact with the scary thing.
- Don't speak in a high-pitched voice and tell him everything is okay, especially if you use "okay" to tell him what he is doing is good behavior in other contexts.

Appendix 7

Hand Targeting

Objective: Your dog touches a target with his nose

Position: Standing and facing your dog

Treats: In your right hand if your dog will be walking on your left side when he is on leash and your left hand if your dog will be walking on your right side when he is on leash.

Definitions

- Storage Hand – the hand that you hold the treats in
- Touch Hand – the hand that is going to be the target hand. If your dog is going to be walking on your left, your touch hand should be your left hand, and vice versa.

If your dog is small or short, you can use a soup ladle or back scratcher instead of your hand so you don't have to bend down so far. Have him touch the ladle/scratcher and put the treats in the ladle/scratcher.

An alternative for a small dog is to teach him on a raised surface such as a table. Be sure to put a rug on the table so he does not slip and also leash him so he cannot fall off.

Prep

- Treats need to be small and SOFT. Don't use hard treats because it takes too long for your dog to chew them.
- Get ALL your treats ready (i.e., easily accessible and cut to size) BEFORE you begin the training. For each lesson, prepare at least 100 treats. You may not use them all, but you don't want to stop in the middle of the session and lose the momentum.
- Remember to cut down his regular food because you're giving him so many treats and you don't want him to put on weight.

Here is a guide for the size of the treats. If you think the sizes described here are too small, remember that your dog can find a crumb on the floor and be ecstatic about it!

- If your dog weighs less than 5 pounds, the treats should be half the size of a grain of rice.
- If your dog weighs 5-10 pounds, the treats should be the size of a grain of rice.
- If your dog weighs 10-25 pounds, the treats should be half the size of a pea.
- If your dog weighs 25-40 pounds, the treats should be half the size of a pea.
- If your dog weighs 40-60 pounds, the treats should be the size of a garbanzo bean.
- If your dog weighs 60-80 pounds, the treats should be a little larger than a raspberry.
- If your dog weighs over 80 pounds, the treats should be the size of an almond with the shell on.

Training

- Take a smelly piece of meat and smear it on the palm and fingers of your touch hand.
- Put the palm of your empty touch hand, fingers facing down, just in front of your dog's nose, no more than ¼" from his nose.
- He will move his head to smell and touch your hand.
- The instant he touches your hand, tell him "yes" or "good dog" and immediately transfer one treat from your Storage Hand to your Touch Hand and let him eat the treat. (I'm going to abbreviate this Y&T, which means transfer the treat from your Storage Hand to your Touch Hand, say "yes" or "good dog" and immediately give him a treat.)

   Deliver the treats from your Touch Hand – it's the same hand he touched. Do not give him the treats from the Storage Hand.

- Repeat these steps at least six times.
- When he is comfortable touching your Touch Hand, say "Touch" *before* you want him to touch it – in other words, he learns how to Touch first and then you add the command.

You made it very easy for him to touch your hand because it was right in front of his nose. Now you are going to make it a bit more difficult.

If you think of the area surrounding your dog's face as a clock, your Touch Hand was at six o'clock.

- Move your Touch Hand to three o'clock so he has to move his head to touch it.
- Repeat at least three times.
- Move your Touch Hand to nine o'clock so he has to move his head to touch it.
- Repeat at least three times.
- Move your Touch Hand slightly forward to he has to take a step to touch it.
- Move your Touch Hand a little bit more forward so he has to take 2 steps to touch it – you will need to back up.
- Then 3 steps, 4 steps, etc.

In a nutshell, the sequence is

1- Move your empty Touch Hand.
2- Say "touch."
3- When he touches, immediately Y&T with your Touch Hand.
4- Then make it a bit harder by moving your hand farther away and then backing up a step at a time.

Now change your position so that your dog is next to you because that is where you ultimately want him to be when he is on leash and you're walking. Reteach the exercise to your dog from the beginning except now, you take one step forward, just as you would when you take him out for his daily walk on leash. Repeat several times. Then take two steps and repeat several times. Then three steps and repeat, etc. Pretty soon, you are walking with your dog by your side while he is targeting your hand. Congratulations!

Uses: Recall, going past scary things on the walk, going closer to scary things – because he focuses on your hand he doesn't focus on the scary thing, walking past distractions, foundation behavior for tricks.

Appendix 8

Handling Exercises to Prepare your Puppy for the Groomer and the Vet

For the Groomer

HANDLING: While you are at home, you can handle your dog as your groomer would. Choose a quiet time and a quiet place, and give him treats during this whole process. Begin by just touching all parts of his body as if you are giving him an all-over body massage. Scratch his tummy, under his chin, and behind his ears. Pet him with long, gentle strokes in the direction his hair grows.

As he becomes comfortable with that, touch his ears, look inside his ears, stroke his muzzle. Pick up his paws, run your hands down his legs, gently squeeze his feet, toes, and tail.

CLIPPING NAILS: Some dogs do not like having their nails clipped. Here's a method to desensitize him to the sound of the clippers and the actual clipping of his nails.

- Hold some wooden matchsticks about a foot away from your dog and cut them with the clippers to get your dog used to the sound, giving him a treat with each cut.
- At other times, handle your dog's feet several times a day, giving him a scrumptious treat as you touch them.
- Then take the nail clipper out and put it on the floor near your dog. Give him a treat every time he looks at the

clipper. Pick it up and slowly bring it closer to him giving him treats the entire time he looks at the clipper.

- Hold your dog's foot and put the matchstick underneath him foot and cut the matchstick.
- When he gets used to this, then put the clipper to his nails and pretend to cut them.
- Then actually cut just the tip of one nail, being careful not to cut into the quick, which is a blood vessel running the length of his nail. If your dog has white nails, you can see where the quick ends. You cannot see it if your dog has black nails. Be *very* careful!
- Be sure not to squeeze his foot when you squeeze the clippers.
- If he is comfortable with that, then cut the tip another nail.

There is no rule that he has to have all his nails cut in one sitting. Cut a couple nails; take a break; then cut a couple more.

THE SOUNDS: The two sounds to get him used to are the sounds of the hair clippers and the dryer. Begin with the dryer. Put the dryer several feet from him. Turn it on and off very quickly. Toss him a treat every time it is on. As he acclimates to the sound, leave it on for a few more seconds and gradually it move closer to him. Remember the treats! When you finally get close to him, let it blow on the least sensitive part of his body (which is probably his back) and give him a treat. Leave it on for longer periods. When he is used to the dryer, repeat the entire process again with an electric razor or other appliance that simulates the sound of hair clippers.

THE TABLE: Get him used to being on a raised surface. Several times a day, pick him up and place him on a table, a countertop, your washer or dryer, or some other raised surface on top of which you have put a rubber mat.

THE CRATE: Make him want to go into the crate. Put his favorite toys in the crate and close the door so he is outside and the toys are inside next to the door. Now he wants to go into the crate to get his toys. Open the door and let him in to get them. Leave the door open. Gradually put them further back so he has to go further inside to get them. Do the same thing with his food, and put his dish further back. Begin swinging the door while he is eating. As he gets accustomed to the noise, then close it for just a short period of time. Slowly lengthen the time the door is closed.

For the Vet

While you are at home, handle your dog as your vet would during an exam. Choose a quiet time and quiet place. Give him treats during this whole process and let him become comfortable with each part of the process before proceeding to the next part.

ELEVATING HIM: Several times a day, pick up your dog and put him on a raised surface such as a countertop so he will not be afraid of getting up on the examination table.

HANDLE HIM ALL OVER: Begin by just touching all parts of his body as if you are giving him an all-over body massage. As he gets comfortable with that, then touch his ears, look inside his ears, open his mouth, touch his teeth and gums as if you were brushing his teeth, move his tongue around. Pick up his paws. Run your hands down his legs. Gently squeeze his feet, toes, and tail. Hold and then gently squeeze his shoulders and then his hips between your hands. Press gently on his spine.

MANIPULATE HIS BODY: Now get him ready for the positions he might be put in. Give him a bear hug while you are facing him. Then give him one from behind him. Hold his head in the crook of your arm. This is how a technician would hold him.

Put him on his right side and stretch his legs out away from you. Then do the same thing on his left side. Lay him on his back and give him a belly rub. Then gently stretch his legs out. These positions simulate positions for x-ray procedures.

Every member of your family should repeat these exercises. Then have someone he knows do the same thing. Remember to give him treats!!!

Resources

List of Dog Trainer Organizations in the United States

Association of Animal Behavior Professionals, http://www.associationofanimalbehaviorprofessionals.com

Association of Professional Dog Trainers, http://apdt.com

Certification Council for Professional Dog Trainers, http://www.ccpdt.org

International Association of Animal Behavior Consultants, http://iaabc.org

National Association of Dog Obedience Instructors, http://nadoi.org

International Association of Canine Professionals, http://canineprofessionals.com

List of Websites

My Sites

http://PuppySocializationGuide.com

http://www.puppy-dog-potty-training.com

http://www.DogBooksLibrary.com

http://www.DogSeminarsDirectory.com

http://www.DoggieManners.com

http://www.TeacupPuppiesAndDogs.com

http://www.DogTrainersDirectory.com

http://www.los-angeles-rescue-dog-adoption.com

Other Sites referred to in **Puppy Socialization: An Insider's Guide to Dog Behavioral Fitness**

AVSAB Position Statement on Puppy Socialization
http://tinyurl.com/q3u6mpz

http://breedingbetterdogs.com/breeding-better-dogs.php

http://www.akc.org

Association of Pet Behavior Counsellors
http://tinyurl.com/ovgl8vv

http://www.dogstardaily.com

www.drfoxvet.com

http://www.foxredlabs.ca

http://www.freshpatch.com/wolff

www.Goldengatelabradoodles.com

Gun Dog Magazine http://tinyurl.com/o4zp2vq

www.hawspets.org

The Kong Company http://tinyurl.com/oq6p4tg

http://www.raisewithpraise.com

http://www.silverkennel.com

http://www.superpuppy.com

Dr. Ed Bailey's articles http://tinyurl.com/lv3362x

www.WoofsofWisdom.com

List of Dog Trainer Organizations in the United States

Association of Animal Behavior Professionals,
http://www.associationofanimalbehaviorprofessionals.com

Association of Professional Dog Trainers, http://apdt.com

Certification Council for Professional Dog Trainers,
http://www.ccpdt.org

International Association of Animal Behavior Consultants,
http://iaabc.org

National Association of Dog Obedience Instructors,
http://nadoi.org

International Association of Canine Professionals,
http://canineprofessionals.com

The websites and organizations listed are for your reference
only. Although portions of the websites were source
materials for this book, their entire content is not endorsed
by the author or publisher. Similarly, every trainer in every
organization listed does not use the same training methods
or adhere to the same training philosophy and is not
endorsed by the author or publisher.

Bibliography

Abrantes, The Evolution of Canine Social Behaviour

Appleby, David, Ain't Misbehavin'

Bailey, Dr. Ed, http://tinyurl.com/lv3362x

Bailey, Gwen, The Ideal Puppy

Bailey, Joan, How to Help Gun Dogs Train Themselves

Bleicher , Sydney and Peggy van Dam, Urban Puppy Toolkit

Burmaster, Corally, The Puppy Headstart Program

Case, Linda P. The Dog – Its behavior, Nutrition & Health

Clark, Gail I., Puppy Parenting

Coppinger, Raymond and Lorna, Dogs: A Startling New Understanding of Canine Origin, Behavior & Evolution

Coren, Dr. Stanley, Why Does My Dog Act That Way?

Dehasse, Dr. Joel, http://tinyurl.com/l5ocgvl

Dodman, Dr. Nicholas, Puppy's First Steps

Dunbar, Dr. Ian, After You Get Your Puppy

Dunbar, Dr. Ian, Puppy Classes Redux DVD

Fox, Dr. Michael W., Understanding Your Dog

Fox, Dr. Michael W., Superdog

Hangren, Anders, Stress, Anxiety and Aggression in Dogs

Hancock, Judith M., Puppy Journal

Handelman, Barbara, Canine Behavior: A Photo Illustrated Handbook

Hetts, Suzanne, PhD., and Estep, PhD, Daniel Q., Raising a Behaviorally Healthy Puppy

Hope, Jerry, The Breeder's Guide to Raising Superstar Dogs

Laurence, Kay, Learning About Dogs – Learning Games

Leeds, Joshua, and Wagner DVM, MS Susan, Through a Dog's Ear

Lindsay Steven R., Handbook of Applied Dog Behavior and Training

McGreevy, PHD., MRCVS, Paul, A Modern Dog's Life

Overall, Karen, Clinical Behavioral Medicine for Small Animals

Owens, Paul, The Puppy Whisperer

Pfaffenberger, Clarence, The New Knowledge of Dog Behavior

Randolph, Elizabeth, How to Help Your Puppy Grow Up to be a Wonderful Dog

Sauter, Frederic J. and Glover, John A., Behavior, Development, and Training of the Dog

Scidmore, Brenda K, and McConnell, PhD, Patricia B, Puppy Primer

Shumannfang, Barbara, Puppy Savvy

Scott, John Paul and Fuller, John L, Genetics and the Social Behavior of the Dog

Tellington-Jones, Linda, The Tellington Touch [aka Ttouch]

Wood, Deborah, Help for Your Shy Dog

Made in the USA
Columbia, SC
07 October 2020